International Perspectives
on Mental Health

International Perspectives on Mental Health

Critical Issues across the Lifespan

Barbara Fawcett

Zita Weber

and

Sheila Wilson

palgrave
macmillan

First published 2012 by
PALGRAVE MACMILLAN

Palgrave Macmillan in the UK is an imprint of Macmillan Publishers Limited, registered in England, company number 785998, of Houndmills, Basingstoke, Hampshire RG21 6XS.

Palgrave Macmillan in the US is a division of St Martin's Press LLC, 175 Fifth Avenue, New York, NY 10010.

Palgrave Macmillan is the global academic imprint of the above companies and has companies and representatives throughout the world.

Palgrave® and Macmillan® are registered trademarks in the United States, the United Kingdom, Europe and other countries.

ISBN 978–0–230–22248–9

This book is printed on paper suitable for recycling and made from fully managed and sustained forest sources. Logging, pulping and manufacturing processes are expected to conform to the environmental regulations of the country of origin.

A catalogue record for this book is available from the British Library.

A catalog record for this book is available from the Library of Congress.

10   9   8   7   6   5   4   3   2   1
21 20 19 18 17 16 15 14 13 12

Printed and bound in Great Britain by the MPG Books Group, Bodmin and King's Lynn

Contents

v

Part III Mental Health Landscapes

Acknowledgements

Sheila Wilson would like to acknowledge her husband, Malcolm; her parents, Alasdair and Margaret; her sisters, Susan and Fiona; her son, Jett; and her daughter, Skye. Zita Weber would like to dedicate this book to her grandparents and parents, and Barbara Fawcett would like to thank her husband, Maurice and daughters, Katie and Sophie for their ongoing perseverance.

About the Authors

Barbara Fawcett is Professor of Social Work and Policy Studies in the Faculty of Education and Social Work at the University of Sydney, Australia. Previously she was Head of the Department of Applied Social Science and Humanities at the University of Bradford where she is now Honorary Research Professor. Prior to entering the University of Bradford, she spent 13 years in the field. Her research interests focus on mental health, disability, women and violence, participative action research and postmodern feminism.

Previous and current books include:

Fawcett, B., Goodwin, S. Meagher, G. and Phillips, R. (2010) *Social Policy for Social Change*.

Fawcett, B. and Waugh, F. (2008) *Addressing Violence, Abuse and Oppression: Debates and Challenges*.

Fawcett, B. and Karban, K. (2005) *Contemporary Theory, Policy and Practice in Mental Health*.

Fawcett, B., Featherstone, B. and Goddard, J. (2004) *Contemporary Child Care Policy and Practice*.

Fawcett, B. (2000) *Feminist Perspectives on Disability*.

Fawcett, B. Featherstone, B., Fook, J. and Rossiter, A. (2000) (eds) *Research and Practice in Social Work: Postmodern Feminist Perspectives*.

Fawcett, B., Featherstone, B., Hearn, J. and Toft, C. (1996) (eds) *Violence and Gender Relations: Theories and Interventions*.

Dr Zita Weber is an honorary lecturer at the University of Sydney, Australia, where she taught for 20 years. Prior to entering academia, she was a social work practitioner in mental health, child health and rehabilitation areas. Zita has written numerous academic papers and co-authored *Skills for Human Service Practice* (2006, with Agi O'Hara). In addition, Zita has written books about depression and loss and grief for the general public. Some of her titles include *Back from the Blues* (1997), *Out of the Blues* (2000) and *Good Grief* (2001).

Sheila Wilson has worked as a mental health clinician for 15 years and currently serves in a management capacity focusing on service development in the community context. She has operated as a tutor in skills-based subjects and student placements for seven years at the University of Sydney, Australia.

Introduction

As authors, we all have substantial experience of working in the broad arena that comprises the mental health field, and our purpose in writing this book is to trace the development of current theory, policy and practice by looking at historical frameworks, at power relationships and at how knowledge in this complex and highly charged area has evolved. Over time, we have watched the ebb, flow and circularity of a variety of trends and we want to draw attention to the importance of maintaining a constructive, but questioning, outlook. As part of this process, we acknowledge the insights of Peter Beresford when he speaks out about how people's complex experiences and feelings can all too easily be compressed to 'fit' into neatly labelled boxes, how all these boxes can carry with them negative and disempowering connotations and how basic human needs, relating to hope, to meaning and the need to make interpersonal connections, can all too easily be overlooked.

We appreciate that those working within the field of mental health are continually bombarded with new directives and are charged with a bewildering array of responsibilities which include protecting the public, upholding human rights, working with families, working with severe mental distress, incorporating the views of consumers and service users, operating within an evidence base and making underfunded systems work. We have written this book for all those who work within or have contact with mental health systems, and our aim is to facilitate and give space for reflection and analysis. We want to enable readers to step back and review the big picture, to pose critical questions and to identify creative opportunities.

Mental well-being is complex. Our sense of self is influenced by social experiences, by ideological constructions, by prevailing views and by the meanings which we variously ascribe to all these areas. The accounts of those who use mental health services vary enormously. Anecdotally and in terms of the literature and research studies that we refer to throughout this book, there are those who have found an illness model and accompanying treatment programmes helpful and supportive. There are others whose contact with mental health services has promoted avoidance or the exploration of different responses. There are also some who talk of the prevalence of systemic racism or sexism and yet more who point to how experiential knowledge is disregarded. They highlight an overall lack of respect and of experiencing feelings of disempowerment. Clearly, services and support systems vary widely, and it is neither possible nor desirable to create binaries by setting the views of those who use services, against those who work within them. We are all subject to forms of mental distress and throughout there are a diverse range of perspectives, concerns and beliefs operating. There are psychiatrists who focus on the importance of context and meanings in understanding distress, who critically interrogate the use of power and control in mental health services and who continuously appraise the ethical issues involved when psychiatry is used as a form of technology. There are those who use services, as well as pressure groups comprising family members, who rigorously resist any challenge to mental distress being viewed and responded to as anything other than an illness. What we want to do in this book is to further open up debate and discussion and to direct a critical yet creative lens towards policy and practice.

Before moving on to give an overview of the book, it is important to review terminology. Terms employed include madness, mental health, mental ill-health, mental illness, mental distress, medicalization, psychiatry, psychosis and alienation. All of these designations have current relevance, with some being more pertinent in particular contexts. In this book, we use the terms most appropriate to the topic being discussed, but we also explore meaning-making and consider how at particular points certain terms have emerged as being of particular significance.

In Chapter 1, we look at history as comprising not the past, but rather versions of the past. We highlight that historical moments are embedded within socio-cultural contexts and that the importance of context, in terms of social, political and cultural factors, cannot be overstated. As such, context remains central to our understandings of mental well-being and mental ill-health and influences not only how apparently standardized trends such as deinstitutionalization are viewed, but also how our understandings change and evolve. These themes run throughout the book, and in Chapter 2 we reflect on constructions of mental illness and the ways in which understandings about mental health and the policy and practice landscape have been beset by tension and debate. We highlight that policy and practice are partly shaped by the ways in which mental distress and mental ill-health and illness are constructed at particular historical junctures and that this results in the terminology remaining contestable and as always open to interpretation.

In Chapter 3, we explore the influence and impact of mental health legislation and review how this can differ, not only from country to country, but also in Australia, from state to state. We examine the various ways in which mental health laws provide both the context and the basis for decision-making and service delivery, and we consider the influence of human rights concerns and ethical considerations within legislative frames. Accordingly, we acknowledge that well-crafted mental health legislation can operate as a protective factor for those vulnerable to stigma, discrimination and marginalization and that it can also provide the means for ensuring that minimum standards are maintained both in hospital and within community contexts. However, we also draw attention to how the legal framework can be experienced as oppressive, and as eroding, rather than safeguarding, human rights. In this chapter, we pay attention to the underlying rationales for mental health legislation, we consider issues of implementation and we appraise general principles and the underpinning value systems which govern responses to those diagnosed with mental disorders.

In Chapter 4, we direct attention towards the increasing numbers of children worldwide who are being diagnosed with mental health conditions. The reasons given for the rising statistics include increased 'stressors' such as the pressure to achieve, to maintain credibility with peers and to manage a range of adverse experiences, and these are explored in detail. However, whilst taking account of these considerable pressures, we appraise the increase in the diagnosis of conditions such as Attention Deficit Hyperactivity Disorder (ADHD) and examine the controversy about whether the statistics represent a marked rise in the numbers of children actually experiencing mental ill-health or whether the situation is more complex and that more children, for variety of reasons, are being regarded or constructed as experiencing an increasing range of disorders. In this chapter, we broaden the discussion relating to children and mental health, and we review the appropriateness and viability of current provision.

In Chapter 5, we continue to explore the issues raised in Chapter 4, but direct our attention towards young people and focus on listening to their voices about what they say they want and would find useful. Young people comprise a service user/consumer group at a critical life stage who are frequently excluded from discussions about their understandings, experiences or views of services and who have not, to date, had a distinctive voice in the debates surrounding mental health. This stands alongside services which are described as overloaded, fragmented and which, according to many young people, do not meet their needs. In this chapter, we explore the mounting pressures for a greater range of holistic support services that focus on strengths and which fully involve young people. We also appraise the challenges faced by professionals working in this complex and highly charged arena.

In Chapter 6, both policy and practice relating to adults are subject to critical review in historical as well as in contemporary contexts. We explore factors associated with gender, ethnicity and 'race', and – as in other chapters – we pay attention to rising statistics and to causational as well as to constructionist forms of explanation. In this chapter, we highlight the demands placed on mental health professionals and draw attention to the importance of maintaining an awareness of the social context of people's lives as well as their biographies and personal narratives. In other chapters, and particularly in Chapter 10, we take this discussion further and look at how a form of spatial analysis linked to social entrepreneurship can contribute to innovation in this field.

In Chapter 7, we explore the issues and challenges facing older people in the rocky terrain of mental health and later life, and we review policy and practice in relation to a life stage which generally receives minimal attention. As we argue throughout this book, health, which includes mental health and wellbeing, is both multidimensional and holistic, incorporating a wide range of factors. These clearly relate to socio-economic influences, lifespan issues and personalized quality of life perspectives. In this chapter, we emphasize that older women and men generally have also to contend with age-related inequality, increased experiences of age-related loss and changing life patterns. These in turn are affected by levels of social and financial security, family support and what is increasingly being referred to as resilience. Different discourses of welfare and mental health have positioned older people in a number of ways, inevitably influencing experiences and perceptions. In this chapter, we consider the importance of place, the different ways in which older people are constructed in relation to mental health issues and welfare discourses generally, and the obvious tensions between considerations of 'risk' and safety *and* self-determination and emotional well-being.

In Chapter 8, we examine the concept of 'dual diagnosis' and explore how this term has gained considerable currency within clinical psychiatric practice in Western nations over recent years. Although overall within the book we direct a critical lens towards dominant clinical and psychiatric understandings, in this chapter we recognize that 'dual diagnosis' has obtained an operational identity. We therefore pay attention to definitional issues as well as review the significance of this framework for practice. As part of this process, we consider the tensions that arise in relation to service user or consumer perspectives and subject the challenges posed by the concept of 'dual diagnosis' for socially orientated understandings of mental health to critical scrutiny.

In Chapter 9, we acknowledge that 'caring' not only describes what a person does but also draws attention to a concept which is given meaning through policy documents, practice directives and by means of a variety of interactions between different family members. 'Caring' within families can refer either singly or collectively at different points in time to the presence or absence of emotional ties, to notions of duty that members have for each other and to the provision of a range of forms of support or assistance. 'Caring' can also imply the operation of power imbalances and can carry with it the assumption that certain members are more competent than others. In this chapter, we review the concept of 'caring' from individualized and social perspectives and highlight the tensions embedded in a concept which, although often presented as straightforward and unidimensional, is extremely complex. In all of this, we clearly recognize that families under stress and experiencing distress often require external support. However, we maintain that the form that this takes has to be flexible, well resourced and collaborative as well as responsive and inclusive.

In Chapter 10, we appraise the dynamic nature of mental well-being and mental health in relation to the constantly changing interaction between an individual and their environment. We pay particular attention to the challenges faced by mental health professionals, and we appraise the significance of operating principles associated with anti-discriminatory and anti-oppressive practice and critical reflection. We also subject the opportunities and constraints provided by social inclusion agendas to critical scrutiny. As part of this process, we look at how the current emphasis on social inclusion can be used to further open up policy and practice spaces for analysis and action by mental health professionals, and we explore the utility for practice of flexible community-orientated tools such as spatial analysis and social entrepreneurship.

Throughout the book, we do not underestimate the difficulties faced by mental health professionals operating in situations beset by scarce resources and prescriptive procedures. Rather, what we seek to do is to emphasize opportunities and to explore the ways in which professionals and consumers/service users can work together. As part of this process we emphasize that a key challenge relates to how to be constructively critical and reflective whilst simultaneously remaining engaged with the day-to-day realities of policy and practice. This often involves combining the aspirational with the routine and the inspirational with the negative effects of what frequently appears to be systemic inertia.

In all of the chapters, we explore the contribution that can be made by different understandings of mental health and well-being, and we look at how different perspectives can direct an illuminating gaze towards dominant discourses. Clearly, medical models and psychiatric understandings do not remain static and cannot be artificially unified and used as monolithic targets. We do not intend to establish a new structure. Instead, we direct attention towards deconstructing taken-for-granted perspectives, to exploring how power/knowledge differentials operate in different circumstances and to an examination of the contribution made by prevailing value systems. We also consider the influence of structural factors, such as poverty and endemic violence, on the mental health of individuals and families, and we appraise the contribution both now and in the future that can be made by communities, with community defined to incorporate geographical communities and communities of interest as well as communities forged by alienation.

Our aim in this book is to continue to broaden, rather than to narrow, the discussion about what mental health is and to explore opportunities as well as to appraise constraints. As a result, part of this process has involved questioning an enduring emphasis on individual pathology and biological determinism and appreciating and fully acknowledging diverse knowledge frames which importantly include experiential knowledge. We embrace and acknowledge complexity and draw attention to the dangers involved in reducing multi-faceted situations to one or two apparently noteworthy factors and to straightforwardly making everything fit together. We are aware that we present many challenges, but for everyone involved in the arena of mental health, from consumers/service users to a range of professionals, the refrain 'this could be so much better' has a familiar resonance. Clearly, there will be different views about what changes are required, but we argue that it is only by broadening perspectives and engaging in critical but constructive debates that this refrain can be positively addressed.

PART I

Mental Health: An Overview

CHAPTER 1

Historical Moments in Mental Health: From Straitjackets to the Streets

History, according to Liam Clarke (2004), is not the past, but rather versions of the past. When we apply this premise to the history of madness, psychiatry, power and knowledge, it is clear that there is not just one version of the past, but many. Historical moments, just like contemporary situations, are clearly embedded within socio-cultural contexts and the importance of context cannot be overstated. It cannot be assumed, for example, that given the social, political, cultural and infrastructural differences between countries, similar responses to interventions will follow (Beukens et al., 2004). Bracken and Thomas (2001), two leading psychiatrists, reinforce this point when they state that 'Contexts, that is to say social, political and cultural realities, should be central to our understanding of madness' (2001: 727).

Given the importance of contextual sensitivity, any analysis of historical narratives across the world will clearly offer points of convergence as well as points of divergence and difference in theories, policies and practices. Deinstitutionalization, which has become an almost international phenomenon, for instance, has been interpreted locally in different countries and case management, a ubiquitous term that has accompanied deinstitutionalization, is practised within a local context.

Even a cursory glance at the historical moments in relation to mental distress, mental health and mental illness reveals instances of beliefs moving beyond the available evidence, some theories becoming more and more questionable, whilst certainties occlude the complexities of the context (Hatfield and Lefley, 1993; Fawcett and Karban, 2005). As Clare (1983) concludes, speculation in understanding the nature of mental ill-health or illness often masquerades as scientific truth. Fernando (2002) claims that although Western psychiatry prides itself on being rational and scientific, to an outsider from a non-Western perspective, it is difficult to deduce the underlying belief system and to appreciate its theoretical basis. This notion of looking at something from the 'inside' or the 'outside' highlights how the perspective adopted will expose different understandings of mental health and mental distress and illness and forms of psychiatry. In some cultures, for example, Asian, African and South American, there may be less concern about and even active promotion of different states of consciousness, as compared to Western culture. What may be considered 'abnormal' experiences indicating symptoms of illness in the West may be interpreted by some non-Europeans as varieties of positive inner experiences (Fernando, 2002). Moreover, the boundaries between mind and body, health and illness are drawn differently in different cultural traditions (Fernando, 2002). In cross-cultural contexts, there may be differences in understandings of mental health and resulting gaps in communication between mental health service providers and consumers (Yurkovich and Lattergrass, 2008). Cultural diversity, if not acknowledged and addressed, can lead to the two parties coming from vastly different directions, and at times, literally using different words for certain similar experiences (Spector, 2003).

Historical mental health narratives and other constructions

When we look at dominant mental health narratives, we see that the 1970s saw the beginning of deinstitutionalization with policies of confining those diagnosed as having a mental illness being reversed and community care being promoted (Shorter, 2006). In some countries, such policy directions, in the light of the lack or insufficiency of accompanying resources, have clearly resulted in difficulties for many (Lamb and Bachrach, 2001). However, we can see that these policies have served to focus attention on increased citizenship participation and on greater

human rights protection for people diagnosed with a mental illness (Morrall and Hazelton, 2004; Hazelton, 2005). In the span
of a century and a half, emphasis has shifted from the asylum with its historical legacy of straitjackets, bleeding, purging,
leeches, baths and perforating the scalp (Rice, 1988) to important declarations of rights. In 1992, for example, the United
Nations General Assembly passed Resolution 46/129 on the Protection of Persons with Mental Illness and the Improvement of
Mental Health Care (United Nations General Assembly, 1992).
In 2001, the World Health Organization (WHO) stated that mental health policy and programmes should promote the right to
equality and non-discrimination; the right to privacy, to individual autonomy, to physical integrity; the right to information and
participation; and the right to freedom of religion, assembly and
movement (WHO, 2001). Several commentators have pointed
out that international human rights bodies were initially slow to
apply general human rights protections to the mental health field
(Gostin and Gable, 2004; Rosenthal and Sundram, 2004; Carney,
2008). There has also been criticism that national or state mental health legislation invariably overrides human rights legislation
(Spandler and Carlton, 2009). However, notwithstanding these
points, the extension of international human rights treaties into
the realm of mental health can be seen to have affected the direction of national mental health policies (Rees, 2003; Gostin and
Gable, 2004; Carney, 2008). In many countries, safeguarding and
enhancing the rights of people with a diagnosis of mental illness is
considered central to service delivery and important for continu-
ous quality development and improvement within mental health
services (Hazelton and Clinton, 2002; Sharma, 2003). However,
it is important to note that although some commentators point to
the ways in which mental health legislation in Western nations
in particular has managed to balance rights between those of
an individual assessed as experiencing a mental disorder or illness and the general public (Whiteford et al., 2000), others have
argued that in order to advance a human rights approach to mental health policy, the reigning bio-medical orthodoxies inherent in
prevailing policy and practice have to be challenged to open up
space for the availability of alternatives (Lewis, 2009; Spandler
and Carlton, 2009).

   In terms of policy, Grob, writing about the US experience,
has maintained that 'Rhetoric and ideology shape agendas and

debates; they create expectations that in turn mould policies; and they inform the socialization, training, and education of those in professional occupations' (2008: 98). Fawcett et al. (2011), in turn, draws attention to the concept of 'policy' being highly contested. We particularly focus on the notion of policy as being difficult to encapsulate. This is because it is multifaceted and involves a series of related decisions as well as a number of different people in the policy-making and implementation phases. Rogers and Pilgrim (2001), writing from within the context of the British experience, claim,

> The term mental health policy at the turn of the twenty-first century refers to legal arrangements, policy directives and service investments in relation to the aggregate picture which has accumulated over the past 100 years. It is partly about the control of behaviour, partly about promoting well-being, partly about ameliorating distress and partly about responding to dysfunction.
>
> (2001: 226)

Recent international policy directions have been characterized by concern for the citizenship participation and human rights protection of those in receipt of mental health services. Hazelton (2005) compared recent mental health reforms in four countries – the United Kingdom, Australia, Italy and Brazil – with a particular emphasis on the relationship between deinstitutionalization, citizenship and human rights. His conclusion highlights that whilst in the United Kingdom and Australia recent emphasis has been directed to creating operational improvements in mental health services, scant attention has been paid to evaluating the outcomes of deinstitutionalization in terms of '... improvements in the life circumstances of people diagnosed with mental illness' (2005: 239). By contrast, Hazelton (2005) concludes, in Italy and to some extent in Brazil, much more attention has been devoted to approaching mental health reform as an issue of citizenship and human rights. However, even in these countries, Hazelton could find little evidence of the use of these concepts as the basis for any form of evaluation. In Australia, the two separate instances where two women, Cornelia Rau and Vivian Alvarez (Solon), were inappropriately detained in psychiatric facilities have opened up space for a debate on mental health reform and changes in policy direction. Reform tends to follow scandals, and in Japan, for example, a scandal involving the killing of two inpatients by staff in a psychiatric hospital (Utsunomiya scandal) led to a major revision of the Mental Health Law in 1987 (Law No. 98, 1987). This revision focused on two major features: (1) the protection of human rights for people diagnosed with mental disorders and (2) the provision of rehabilitative services to promote community integration of people with mental disorders (Kuno and Asukai, 2000). In recent years, there have been demands in many countries for mental health services to be evaluated in terms of citizenship and human rights principles (Hazelton, 2005), but so far little overall has been achieved.

Newnes comments, 'The way we tell the histories of psychiatric events, practices and ideas changes over time' (2002: 21). Indeed from the vantage point of contemporary mental health policy and practice, considering a list of historical facts only gives a glimpse of some moments in mental health history, with these also predominantly representing the perspectives of the more powerful players. Historical accounts tend not to uncover the complexities of context, the nuances of practices 'on the ground' or the professional 'din' around various ideologies that have informed understandings about mental health, mental distress and mental illness. Mental health professionals have demonstrated a tendency to favour one particular approach to understanding mental ill-health and this is associated with their professional education and background (Coppock and Hopton, 2000; Lester and Glasby, 2006). With the rise of the consumer movement and the active input of 'carers' over the past few years, the interplay between socio-cultural, environmental and political factors has been highlighted. Consequently, as Tyrer and Steinberg have suggested, 'those who imprison themselves within the confines of one model only have the perspective of the keyhole' (2003: 138).

Within the various and often conflicting histories of psychiatry which have been produced, many have focused on the implications of entrenched power imbalances and gendered or racist responses. Major contributions in this area include the powerful voices of Showalter (1985), Ussher (1991), Faith (1993), Russell (1995) and Fernando (2003), and we will look at these throughout this book. What follows at this point is an unfolding of one version of the historical narrative, amongst the many that comprise what Newnes has called 'the histories of psychiatry' (2002: 7). This narrative looks back to the beginning, moves through the key policy and practice shifts in the twentieth century and arrives at the contemporary point with its challenges for the future. This is a future in which mental health policy and practice increasingly are inviting public dialogue and scrutiny, and are holding a mirror up to their own reflections.

In the beginning

Madness, mental distress, mental ill-health, mental illness, lunacy, insanity, or the term with most context-specific currency, have seemingly been ubiquitous throughout history. In Western culture before the eighteenth century, there were diverse and assorted views about madness and few with any links to medicine (Russell, 1995). From the Middle Ages through to the sixteenth century, beliefs and practices connected madness to religion. Some were seen to be in receipt of divine guidance or inspiration, others as possessed by the Devil or evil spirits. Within European popular imagination, those considered as mad, heretical or otherwise rejecting of dominant beliefs were practitioners such as sorcerers, alchemists, astrologers, magicians and midwives (Porter, 1987; Russell, 1995; Fawcett and Karban, 2005). During the Renaissance, madness was linked to folly, a type of immorality, a human weakness not connected with the Devil. At this point, understandings of madness were divorced from any religious connotations. However, other beliefs were also held which grouped those regarded as mad with those accused of serious immorality. Later, economic forces and cyclical movements in employment ushered in a new era. According to Foucault (1973), in France repressive institutions of detention were established to house beggars, vagabonds, drunks and the insane. Similar institutions were set up in England, Germany, Holland, Italy and Spain, and with this social practice came a new conception of madness (Foucault, 1973). Up until the end of the eighteenth century, these inmates were considered not as mad or criminal, but rather as 'unreasonable'. Those actions, thoughts or states of living that 'went against reason' were considered to be freely chosen and immoral, and madness was only one such state (Russell, 1995). Foucault (1973) pointed out that with the spread of disease in the early nineteenth century, the inmates of the confinement houses were thought to be responsible, just as the image of disease and contamination had been linked with leprosy and leper houses centuries before (Samson, 1995; Fawcett and Karban, 2005). It was this association between disease and the confinement houses that provided doctors with what Russell calls 'an entrance ticket' (1995: 7).

This early foray by medical practitioners into the realm of madness coincided with the rise in the importance of science and a more scientific and less theological understanding of madness. According to Ehreneich and English (1978), it was also a time when, to varying degrees, cultural frameworks in some countries in the world, for example, Britain, parts of Europe, North America and Australia, equated science with goodness and morality.

The opportunity to establish medical practitioners as the 'experts' in the conceptualization and treatment of madness was coupled with and reinforced by concern about increasing their social status (Russell, 1995; Lester and Glasby, 2006). In an editorial from the 1858 issue of the *Journal of Mental Science* (now known as the *British Journal of Psychiatry*), Scull (1979) cites a statement that demonstrates an early medical justification: 'Insanity is purely a disease of the brain. The physician is now the responsible guardian of the lunatic and must remain so.' From around this time, medical doctors entered the field of psychiatry in significant numbers and then turned to the task of developing theories and claiming empirical results to justify their expert position (Russell, 1995). As Samson has suggested, with the rise of the asylum and because psychiatrists were charged with the responsibility of defining and confining patients, psychiatrists could '... effectively create the demand for their own services' (1995: 59).

Institutional impulse

From the early nineteenth century to the mid-twentieth century, across Europe, in the United States, Canada and Australasia, the epoch of institutional mental health care was represented by the asylum or mental hospital, what Goffman calls the 'total institution' (1984: 16). Such establishments were distinguished by high walls, locked doors, seclusion and restraint. Generally speaking, these institutions were large state mental hospitals, each with its own catchment area. This epoch represented a cultural, political and social reflex that made admission to a mental hospital the benchmark of quality mental health care (Porter and

Wright, 2003; Shorter, 2006). In Europe, for the middle and upper classes, spas and sanatoriums were established and became the elective treatment site for 'nervous' illnesses (Shorter, 2006).

Although the efficacy of the asylum would come into question in the history of mental health care, Shorter (2006) points out that, in the early days, 'community' treatment was far more damaging and punitive. Apparently, as late as 1840, those regarded as mad in Denmark were '... locked up in wooden cages in the villages or chained in stalls; 142 such cages were known to officials. As late as 1908 this kind of "community care" was customary in rural Sweden and Finland' (Shorter, 2006: 17). The United States and Europe, in their historical narratives of institutionalization and the practices it condoned, diverge at times in terms of influences, yet converge dramatically in the early twentieth century. Social Darwinism and eugenics were part of American psychiatric history and practice, with California passing a measure for the 'asexualization' of mental patients in 1909 (Fox, 1978). Psychiatry was even used to legitimize slavery in the United States, with claims that black people were relatively free of mental illness, but fell prey to insanity when emancipated (Fernando, 2003). From the late 1890s, laws against marriages between black and white people were widespread (Fernando, 2003), and many states followed the Connecticut example of passing legislation regulating marriages between whites for eugenic purposes (Grob, 1983). However, as Skultans (1979) and Showalter (1985) highlight, 'psychiatric Darwinism' was evident in Britain under the influence of Henry Maudsley, whose work linked hereditary defect with mental disorder, moral impropriety and crime. Neurological surgery, introduced in 1936, controlled the inside body of a mental patient just as institutional segregation controlled them externally within the social environment. In the words of Samson, 'By literally cutting out portions of the brain that are alleged to cause mentally defective conditions, psychosurgeons were, in Foucauldian terms, able to impose "Truth" itself' (1995: 64).

In the Preface of a book titled *The Age of Madness* and edited by Thomas Szasz, he tells the reader that 'Mental hospitalization is not the first, nor probably the last, social intervention which is ostensibly helpful but actually harmful to its supposed beneficiaries' (1973: xii). Part Three of his book is titled 'The Flowering of Psychiatric Power' and includes essays from professionals and consumers about the uses and abuses of psychiatry.

In one essay called 'From the Slaughterhouse to the Madhouse', the originator of electroconvulsive therapy (ECT), Ugo Cerletti, describes his discovery of the use of electric current to immobilize hogs in the slaughterhouse and his subsequent experimentation with patients. In this institutionalized era, scant attention was paid to patients' rights. Indeed, it might be said that Cerletti blatantly ignored one patient's rights – the patient who became the first to receive shock therapy. In his own account, Cerletti does not mention having gained permission from anyone for administering what he knew himself to be experimental. On the grounds that he considered it 'treatment', he administered 110-volt shocks to a patient. In fact, when the patient objected, exclaiming, 'Not another one! It's deadly!' (1973: 155) rather than discontinue, Cerletti administered another shock to him. Cerletti wrote:

> I confess that such explicit admonition under such circumstances, and so emphatic and commanding, coming from a person whose enigmatic jargon had until then been very difficult to understand, shook my determination to carry on with the experiment. But it was just this fear of yielding to a superstitious notion that caused me to make up my mind. The electrodes were applied again, and 110-volt discharge was applied for 0.2 second.
>
> (1973: 155–156)

In the 1970s, such convulsion 'treatment' declined in popularity due to bad press, but enjoyed resurgence in the 1980s and 1990s (Abrams, 1989; Coffey and Weiner, 1990; Frank, 1990).

Psychiatric experimentation can be seen to have continued with other 'treatments' such as those which induced a coma, for instance, in insulin coma therapy, and neurosurgery where surgical removal of part of the brain was performed. In Sydney, Australia, as late as the 1970s, a psychiatrist, Harry Bailey, who was to take his own life when a Royal Commission examined his treatments in a small private institution, practised a form of experimental coma therapy called 'deep sleep'.

The hospital-based approach can be seen to have dominated the delivery of mental health services well into the 1960s in most Western countries. Interestingly, the institutional approach to the management of madness has a longer history, occurring in the Islamic Empire as early as AD 683 in Cairo, Egypt, and by the thirteenth century, there were well-established asylums in the Arab Empire, including in Granada in Spain (Ellenberger, 1974). These Islamic asylums were called 'moristans', and according to Dols although the treatment included physical restraint and beatings, it also focused on the dispensing of medicines, decoration to 'cheer the deranged' and 'music played for their benefit' (1992: 121). Fernando (2003) contends that the Islamic Empire was the first to develop a comprehensive medical approach to madness and to hospitalize people considered to be mad, yet the social position of the moristan in medieval Islamic society was different from the later insane asylums of Europe. The moristans did not function as repositories for what Dols calls 'the "great confinement" of the socially undesirable' (1992: 129). According to Dols, the moristans were small, usually located in the centre of the city, accessible to visitors and 'accepted matter-of-factly' (1992: 128) by society.

Elsewhere in the world, no record exists of this historical institutional impulse. For instance, in most parts of Africa, the family has been, and remains, an important resource for the support and care of people diagnosed with mental illness (Gureje and Alem, 2000). Writing about the history of mental health provision in Hong Kong, Ungvari and Chiu say, 'Unbelievable as it may sound, Hong Kong had neither a mental health service nor a qualified psychiatrist until 1948' (2004: 5). Temporary custodial care was provided in the province of Canton and the first purpose-built psychiatric institution with 1200 beds was opened in 1961. The second institution with a 2000-bed capacity opened in 1980, when, as Ungvari and Chiu (2004) point out, the developed world was busily dismantling such establishments. Since the late 1990s, the total number of psychiatric beds has decreased dramatically and community psychiatry, with an emphasis on primary care psychiatry, has evolved in Hong Kong.

There are countries in Europe where the asylum did not dominate. In Hungary, for instance, non-asylum settings such as general hospitals provided residential care as early as the beginning of the twentieth century. In these general hospital 'psychiatry annexes' were people diagnosed with both chronic and acute mental illness (Shorter, 2006). Rudimentary, yet pioneering community care was provided in Hungary until the 1940s in the practice of 'boarding out' or placing former patients in the homes of private individuals. Similar family care placements, an early form of community integration, with care provided by friends and neighbours in the person's home town, also existed across other countries in Europe. According to Shorter, home care '... spread sooner or later to virtually every European country with the exceptions of the Iberian peninsula and England' (2006: 17).

The beginning of the end of the era of the institutional impulse is a contestable point. However, there is general agreement that from the 1970s onwards, in most Western countries, there was what Shorter calls '... an erasure of the firewall between asylum and the community' (2006: 20). Early indications of a move away from institutions can be seen in the Mental Health Act of 1959 in the United Kingdom, which enshrined deinstitutionalization by emphasizing community care. The Hospital Plan for England and Wales, promulgated by the Ministry of Health in 1961, further called for a big decrease in asylum beds and a corresponding increase in psychiatry beds in general hospitals, along with day hospitals and community services (Shorter, 2006).

Many theories have been forwarded regarding the movement towards deinstitutionalization (Goodwin, 1997; Scull, 1977; Lamb and Bachrach, 2001; Shorter, 2006). Such theories about the antecedents of deinstitutionalization range from the popular one of the development of anti-psychotic medication to those which variously emphasize the development of social psychiatry, the emergence of the civil rights movement, increased community tolerance, fiscal pressure and funding system changes. Deinstitutionalization itself has been defined as '... the replacement of long-stay psychiatric hospitals with smaller, less isolated community-based alternatives for the care of mentally ill people' (Lamb and Bachrach, 2001: 1039).

Towards community care

The early promise of deinstitutionalization offering a smooth passage from the mental hospital to the community, however praiseworthy, has not been achieved in practice (Bachrach, 1986; Thornicroft and Bebbington, 1989; Shorter, 2006). According to Lamb and Bachrach (2001), there are three components to deinstitutionalization: (1) the release of people from hospitals to the community, (2) their diversion from hospital admission and

(3) the development of alternative community services. The latter has tended to be significantly affected by the resources made available and initial beliefs that community care would be a less expensive option have been strongly disproved. Writing from their perspective in the United States, Lamb and Bachrach conclude, 'The greatest problems have been in creating adequate and accessible community resources' (2001: 1039). Similar principles, goals and problems have been witnessed in other Western countries in their attempts to move from the institution into the community.

In 1978, 'Law 180' was approved by the Italian parliament. This law aimed to change radically the architecture of psychiatric care in Italy and had a broad international impact (de Girolamo and Cozza, 2000). Through this reform, which was based on a number of philosophical premises deriving principally from the work of Franco Basaglia and the Psychiatria Democratica movement, emerged the idea that all psychiatric evaluation be voluntary, preferably through a network of new outpatient services and that all newly referred individuals be evaluated and treated in the community (Schepper-Hughes and Lovell, 1986; de Girolamo and Cozza, 2000). This law had several provisions: that no new admissions to mental hospitals would take place, that small psychiatric units be set up in general hospitals, with strict limitations on length of stay, and that 'alternative structures' be established in communities (Barbato, 1998; Jones, 1988). Evaluations of the Italian experiment in community care have been mixed. It appears that the most successful implementation of the law has been in the more affluent north of Italy, especially Trieste where Basaglia practised. Elsewhere in Italy, this experience was not duplicated, and there was uneven application of the law resulting in homelessness and exploitation of ex-patients by private landlords (de Girolamo and Cozza, 2000).

What has been described as 'deinstitutionalization' has had a different emphasis in different countries. In Finland, residential psychiatric care was largely shifted to community general hospitals, and in Denmark principles of community care started to take hold after a 1976 law shifted responsibility for psychiatric hospitals from the state to local government bodies (Shorter, 2006). However, a pertinent statement was made in 1979, at a WHO meeting of national mental health directors: 'There [is] little confidence in the idea that an inpatient psychiatric service based only on a district general hospital could meet all the needs of a sector for inpatient psychiatric care' (WHO, 1978: 9). This highlights that in many instances 'deinstitutionalization' continued to foreground in patient provision but in a changed setting. It also led to repeated claims that not enough inpatient beds were being made available, and it is notable that the Danish Psychiatric Society in 1997, when, responding to the doubling in the suicide rate in Denmark between 1970 and 1987, urgently requested that the government increase the number of psychiatric beds (Munk-Jorgensen, 1999).

Shorter (2006) argues that there is a difference between 'de-asylumizing' residential care and deinstitutionalization. He maintains that psychiatric beds established in general hospitals, in psychogeriatric settings, in private sanatoriums and in some cases in charitable psychiatric hospitals exist to offer temporary asylum for people unable to live in the community. However, despite there being clear differences in scale between the old-style asylums and the smaller, psychiatric clinics and hospital annexes, a number of commentators point to the pervasive influence of institutionalizing practices (Scull, 1981; Fawcett and Karban, 2005). Scull (1981) also maintains that in the early years of deinstitutionalization, a 'new trade in lunacy' was created by the emergence of various commercial 'community care' residential facilities and board and care homes. In the United States, this private sector was seen to represent a 'transinstitutionalization' situation rather than deinstitutionalization (Emerson et al., 1981; Scull, 1981).

Although community care did eventually lead to many innovative and well-supported initiatives outside of hospital settings, charges of serious underfunding were being increasingly sustained and resulted in difficulties being experienced by many. By the 1980s, community care was being linked to increasing homelessness, with some psychiatrists claiming that community mental health had failed and that a return to the state mental hospital was required (Gralnick, 1985, Lamb and Bachrach, 2001). This led to a backlash against community care with many people fearing that people in mental distress would 'fall through the cracks', and not receive the housing and support they needed (Samson, 1995).

It does need to be highlighted that community care, with its emphasis on integration and inclusion, presupposes widespread acceptance by the general community of those people who appear different, and the celebration of such differences and diversity. However, as Prior suggests, people are not accepted '...more openly and readily by the community at large simply because they have a new mailing address' (1993: 192). This statement raises the question about the extent to which those diagnosed with mental illness, particularly those who have been known to mental health services for considerable periods, are excluded from everyday opportunities in terms of housing, employment and leisure. It is not simply a matter of being out of hospital, it also is imperative to be included within society and to be able to function as a member of that society. Sayce has described social exclusion as '...the inter-locking and mutually compounding problems of impairment, discrimination, diminished social role and lack of economic and social participation' (2001:121). This can result in lack of status, joblessness, lack of opportunities to establish a family and small or non-existent social networks with all of these aspects serving to compound discrimination, repeated rejection and the consequent restriction of hopes and expectations.

Some of the key aspects in the social exclusion of people diagnosed with mental illness relate to stereotyping, stigma, discrimination and prejudice. Link and Phelan (2001) have posited that social exclusion is a process which incorporates a number of phases. Initially, an individual is regarded as 'different' with this difference being viewed negatively. This is followed by a 'them' and 'us' separation, where the individual becomes 'the other'. Thirdly and finally, 'they' become the thing that is labelled, so they lose their identity, and move from being a person living with a diagnosis of schizophrenia to a 'schizophrenic'. This process highlights the transition from loss of identity and status to negative discrimination and exclusion. Bracken and Thomas point to the fear of difference and 'otherness' in terms of mental health issues that are given coverage in the media (2005). They claim that negative media representations of consumers, 'carers' and even professionals have a long history and conclude that 'What is clear is that in our society, to be a psychiatric service user is to be regarded as a sort of "second class citizen" ' (2005: 84). Marginalized, poor and vulnerable people, whether this is predicated on gender (Williams and Watson, 1996), ethnicity (Fernando, 2002), class (Pilgrim and Rogers, 1999) or mental illness, are subject to media narratives that do not engage with the full story of their lives and everyday experiences.

Deinstitutionalization and community care clearly do not lead to automatic integration. People who now live in the community might, in a previous era, have lived in long-stay institutions, but their geographical inclusion does not guarantee inclusion in the social life and activities of the wider community in which they live. According to Lester and Glasby (2006), recent public concerns and policy which have focused on safety and risk may well have worked to exacerbate the social exclusion of people living with mental distress and a diagnosed mental health condition. In Britain, this awareness of disadvantage compounded by public attitudes and policy directions has led to a number of positive practices relating to community inclusion. By means of Department of Health directives, the National Service Framework and the Social Inclusion Agenda (e.g. the initial Social Inclusion Unit report on mental health and social exclusion proposed a 27-point action plan involving a range of government departments and other organizations in a concerted effort to challenge attitudes and significantly improve opportunities and outcomes for people diagnosed with a mental illness), systemic moves to oppose stigma and discrimination have taken place (Lester and Glasby, 2006; see also Chapter 10). Voluntary sector organizations and The Royal College of Psychiatrists have also campaigned for better community understanding of mental health issues.

Clearly, it would enhance service delivery immeasurably if all governments with responsibility for mental health service delivery actively encouraged community inclusion. However, a culture of inclusion can only be created if the wider society recognizes inequalities and works towards the well-being and the reduction of exclusion of all its members. Writing about the Australian experience, Hazelton and Clinton comment that despite reforms having been co-ordinated through a National Mental Health Strategy, and implemented through successive five-year plans, there is '... little evidence of progress in combating discrimination and safeguarding the human rights and citizenship entitlements of those with mental illness' (2004: 57). They further argue that failure to provide adequate community services in rehabilitation, housing, employment and community support has added to the stress experienced by individuals and by their family members. In essence, it appears that although the National Mental Health

Strategy has brought gains in terms of voicing concerns and raising awareness of issues, there is little evidence that '...the human rights and citizenship entitlements referred to in policy can be enforced in practice' (2004: 57). The Rudd and later Gillard-led Labor government, as part of its 'Stronger, Fairer Australia' policy (2009/2010), has focused on improving outcomes for people living with mental illness and their 'carers' by means of stronger community support programmes, improved employment assistance and increases in overall funding. However, as highlighted earlier, little emphasis has been placed on evaluating these programmes in relation to citizenship and human rights issues.

Concluding remarks

In this chapter, we have traced historical moments in relation to theory, policy and practice and have highlighted opportunities and constraints. In Chapter 2, the narrative continues with reflections on the constructions of mental illness. As part of this process, we explore the diverse and dominant proposals and counter-proposals on the nature of mental illness and offer insights on the competing versions of history.

Constructions of Mental Illness: From the Past towards the Future

As we have seen in Chapter 1, interpretations of mental health and the policy and practice landscape have been fraught with tensions and debates. These relate to different conceptualizations about what constitutes mental health or mental well-being and, in turn, mental ill-health or mental distress. Returning to the emphasis placed by Bracken and Thomas (2001) on the centrality of context, policy and practice can be seen to be influenced by how mental distress and mental ill-health and illness are constructed at any particular point in time. As a result, terms such as mental health, mental distress, mental illness, mental disorder, mental health problems and the associated challenges posed remain contestable.

Challenging and changing constructions of mental illness

Theoretical frameworks wax and wane in popularity and inform the perspective adopted when considering the nature of mental health and mental distress and illness. A question that can be posed is 'Does a biomedical, psychological or sociological framework underpin the definitions and contribute towards particular kinds of policy and service delivery?' Fawcett and Karban (2005) argue that exploring 'a wide range of theoretical perspectives' has clear advantages (2005: 12). Recent theoretical frameworks have included the social model of disability, which argues that it is not an 'impairment' that disables but exclusionary and discriminatory social, economic and political practices which deny civil rights (Oliver, 1983; Oliver and Sapey, 2006). A social causation approach seeks to highlight the interaction between social disadvantage and mental disorder (Golightley, 2006), whilst social constructionist perspectives critically interrogate taken-for-granted assumptions (Horwitz, 2002). Deinstitutionalization, the emergence of community care, research with those with personal experience of mental health systems and material produced by service user and survivor movements can be seen to have paved the way for the critical interrogation of medicalized diagnosis and treatment models and for the reworking of the notion of 'recovery'. Rather than referring to the negation of problematic symptoms, this term has been re-defined to move away from personhood being reduced to a series of problems, to the rediscovery of personal identity, meaning, self-esteem and hope for the future. Patricia Deegan, a pioneering mental health consumer, talks about recovery as 'lived experience in gaining a new and valued sense of self and purpose' (1988: 15). Williams (2002) argues that in terms of social inequalities and mental health it is our challenge to transform the knowledge base, and also to consider the current limitations. She claims that we need to develop '... an inclusive literature that accommodates all people who are damaged by the existence of social inequalities – not just those who have achieved a strong collective voice, or attracted powerful advocates' (2002: 43). Going even further, she suggests that research and literature need integration as much of our knowledge base has been developed along single dimensions such as gender, race, sexuality, class and age. Whilst all these literatures recognize the complexity of oppression, it is time to develop more elaborate analyses, and to create opportunities for bringing together these different domains into a more coherent picture (Williams, 2002).

Bracken and Thomas (2001) emphasize that recent work by medical anthropologists and philosophers further highlights the values and assumptions that underpin psychiatric classifications. They maintain that 'All medical practice involves some negotiation about assumptions and values' (2001: 726), and therefore mental health frameworks should work towards an ethical rather than a technological orientation. They warn of the dangers of not incorporating disparate views, values and assumptions, particularly given the diverse societies in which we now live. In Bradford, for instance, Bracken and Thomas state that the Bradford Home Treatment Service has worked towards keeping values to the fore and has striven to avoid a Eurocentric notion of health, illness and healing. Lewis (2006) believes that mainstream knowledge acts in the interests of the dominant group and stresses that knowledge production cannot exclude the voices of consumers.

Literary interpretations

In literature, there have been many famous depictions of madness, from Shakespeare to the writings of former patients and survivors of the psychiatric hospital system like Sylvia Plath (*The Bell Jar*), Janet Frame (*An Angel at My Table*) and Susanna Kaysen (*Girl, Interrupted*). Joseph Heller in *Catch-22* (1961) captures the contradictions and paradoxes of 'normal' versus 'abnormal' behaviour. In his novel, Yossarian, a fighter pilot, valuing his life, requests he be relieved of flying extra bombing missions on the grounds of being crazy. Heller writes: 'There was only one catch and that was Catch-22 ... Orr would be crazy to fly more missions and sane if he didn't, but if he was sane he had to fly them. If he flew them he was crazy and didn't have to; but if he didn't want to he was sane and had to.' Clarke (2004) points out that Yossarian's predicament mirrors those of people who enter a psychiatric facility but when subsequently they want to leave are prevented from doing so by the imposition of a holding power.

Constructions of mental illness relate to context and culture. Szasz (1970) noted the extensive medicalizing of social issues and personality characteristics in the work of Benjamin Rush, a signatory to the Declaration of Independence and regarded as the father of American psychiatry. Rush, for instance, believed that opposition to the American Revolution, atheism and non-belief in the powers of medicine were signs of mental illness. For Rush, madness was an arterial disease rooted in the blood vessel of the brain and remedies included blood-letting, purgatives, emetics and mechanical devices to tranquilize the patient (Szasz, 1970).

A growing body of literature has highlighted the notion of individualistic and collectivist cultures and their implications for policy formation and service delivery (Triandis, 1995; Westermeyer and Janca, 1997). In essence, individualistic cultures give primacy to individual rights and boundaries, conceptualizing each person as a separate entity from the wider group. Collectivist or sociocentric cultures, on the other hand, focus on family and group membership and social role obligations. Moreover, there is considerable research suggesting that the person's cultural context will inform the experiences of a diagnosed illness. In the case of schizophrenia, for example, culture has been seen to affect self-perception, interpersonal relationships, role acceptance and prognosis (Lefley, 1990; Jablensky et al., 1991). Westermeyer and Janca (1997) have also found that cultural norms can affect social policy and service delivery in terms of issues such as confidentiality and the rights of persons diagnosed with mental illness.

Having knowledge of cultural differences in worldviews and understandings of mental health and mental illness is imperative when mental health professionals work cross-culturally (Fernando, 2002; Vicary and Westerman, 2004; Yurkovich and Lattergrass, 2008). Blanchard (2006), writing from the perspective of an Australian Indigenous woman, who is also a researcher and lecturer, recommends deconstructing the power of stereotypes concerning Aboriginal people and emphasizes the importance of cultural understandings.

Research by Vicary and Westerman (2004), carried out with Aboriginal people in Western Australia, has highlighted how 'longing for, crying for, or being sick for country' has followed the removal of a person from their place of dreaming, or spirit for extended periods of time. They note the limitations contained in classifying such distress as clinical depression.

In their research, Yurkovich and Lattergrass (2008) found that listening to the voices of Native American Indians experiencing mental distress was essential for effective service delivery. For Native American Indians, spirituality is the key to life, with a human/spirit focus informing the complexity of health and illness, represented by the American Indian Medicine Wheel. These respondents told the researchers, 'We are spiritual beings on an earthly journey' and 'We are all spirits wrapped in different robes' (2008: 455). Yurkovich and Lattergrass refer to the centrality of spirituality making it imperative that Native Healers become integral to responding to forms of mental distress. Yip (2004) describes how in contemporary times, Taosim still has an influence on Chinese people's ideas about mental health.

In contrast with Western concepts of health, Taoism advocates self-transcendence, integration with the Law of Nature, inaction and an infinite frame of reference instead of social attainment, self-development, progressive endeavour and personal interpretation. It seems that in traditional Chinese writings, there is no exact word that equates to 'mental health', instead there are words that build a picture of health, such as happiness, harmony, internal sense of security and a relaxed state (Yip, 2004). Yip points out that age, gender, knowledge and experiences of Chinese culture are all factors that may make a difference to an individual's interpretation of traditional Chinese cultural and spiritual beliefs, and that differences are likely to emerge between individuals from the same cultural background.

From an international perspective, the majority of people experiencing forms of mental distress are treated by folk healers and other indigenous practitioners (Fernando, 2002). Such practitioners work from a non-Western belief system that is not predicated on assumptions about the clear separation of the mind and body. According to Capra (1982), these practitioners are informed by traditional wisdom which relates the distress to the whole person, taking account not only of social context but also the influence of the cosmos and the deities.

Williams points out that social inequalities and mental distress are linked, and following Brown (1992), Baker-Miller (1976) and Williams et al. (1993) he argues that some behaviours that are defined as symptoms and disorders are best understood as '...creative responses to difficult personal and social histories, rooted in a person's experience of oppression(s)' (2002: 31). In a similar vein, Fernando (2003) raises the notion of how marginalized people cope with, for instance, racism. Grier and Cobbs (1969) in their book *Black Rage* describe the "'healthy' cultural paranoia" shown by African-American people in the face of widespread racism in the United States. More recently, Franklin (2003) highlights that young African-Americans demonstrate what he calls 'healthy suspiciousness' as a way of surviving. As Fernando comments (2003), failure to consider the context in which seemingly paranoid behaviour is being demonstrated militates against a holistic understanding. It also fails to appreciate what Williams et al. (1993) have labelled the 'creative response' to experiences of oppression.

Proposals and counter-proposals

Proposals and counter-proposals as to the nature of mental distress have emerged from within and outside of psychiatry over the years. Over a span of some 40 years, anti-psychiatry has given way to a resurgence in biomedicine, which in turn is challenged by the notion of postpsychiatry. In the 1960s, counter-proposals about the nature of mental illness grew from within psychiatry. R.D. Laing, who came to symbolize what was called 'anti-psychiatry', in his book *The Divided Self* (1959) critiqued the prevailing biomedical understanding of mental illness and rejected positivism as a philosophy of science. According to Laing, positivism objectifies human experience, by attempting to use the methods of the natural sciences to explore subjective states. Consequently, positivism leads to a perception of 'the patient' as a depersonalized thing, rather than a person. Laing notes that this depersonalization can reproduce some of the features specified as signs and symptoms of mental illness (Laing, 1959: 23, 1982: 31). In Laing's words, 'objective psychiatry is an unobjective attempt to control largely non-objective events by objective means' (1982: 41). Laing believed that the very act of diagnosis created a gulf between different kinds of human experience and, subsequently, between doctor and patient. For Laing, this gulf served to justify what he considered indignities to patients in the name of science and treatment.

Aaron Esterson, working with Laing, conducted research with 11 young females diagnosed with schizophrenia and their families. In *Sanity, Madness and the Family* (1964), they attempted to make intelligible what orthodox psychiatrists saw as a form of nonsense. Going even further, Laing and David Cooper attempted to dissolve the boundary between madness and sanity and to reverse the hierarchical relationship between the two states. Sanity was attacked and insanity elevated in Laing's *The Politics of Experience* (1967) and Cooper's *Psychiatry and Anti-Psychiatry* (1967).

Thomas Szasz, like Laing, has been identified with anti-psychiatry. Szasz, however, did not personally identify with the anti-psychiatry movement as his critique of psychiatry is based on civil libertarian principles. In *The Myth of Mental Illness* (1961), Szasz forwards the notion that mental illness is only illness by way of metaphor. To Szasz, mental illness is a myth fabricated by psychiatrists in order to gain professional power and advancement and is endorsed by the wider society as a means of controlling people who present problems. Szasz contends that psychiatry is a continuation of religious and superstitious concepts of heresy. Mental illness, then, is nothing more than an individual deviation from the social norm, and psychiatrists have placed themselves in a powerful position where society has entrusted them with the enforcement of these social norms. For Szasz, psychiatry is political and the result is '... the systematic use of force and fraud, disguised by the architecture of hospitals and clinics, the rhetoric of healing and the prestige of the medical profession' (1970: 30).

In the United States, in particular, the civil libertarian ideas expressed by Szasz have informed social movements for consumers' rights. The landmark consumers' rights manifesto, *On Our Own* by Judi Chamberlin (1978), draws heavily on ideas from Szasz.

In *Against Therapy* (1988), Jeffrey Masson, like Szasz, directly confronts psychiatry and psychotherapy. Psychiatric and other therapy modes, according to Masson, involve domination, dishonesty and often sexual and physical abuse, all of which masquerade as care and benevolence. Another American psychiatrist, Peter Breggin (1979, 1983, 1991), has written extensively challenging psychiatric intervention, in particular the toxic effects of many of the major neuroleptic drugs as well as electroconvulsive therapy (ECT).

All of these proponents questioned the validity of the concept of mental illness and the benevolence of psychiatric interventions. However, despite such critiques, the biomedical model, with its assumption of biological and scientific foundations, has continued to be regarded by many psychiatrists as the only valid approach in psychiatry (Brown, 1985; Guze, 1989). Nevertheless the anti-psychiatry movement highlighted the power imbalances between mental health professionals and service users and the potential for coercion, surveillance and regulation.

Although there were differences within the largely professionally led anti-psychiatry movement, the main proponents' voices were heard and their messages conveyed beyond professional circles into the general public. Some of them, like Laing, achieved celebrity status, and the message that mental health professionals should move to a model which respects the voices of individuals experiencing distress was strongly argued (Clarke, 2004).

However, despite the force of the anti-psychiatry movement, its influence in policy circles was relatively limited (Lester and Glasby, 2006).

In 1991, a British consultant psychiatrist, Harold Bourne, called for a reconstruction of psychiatry to '...make it relevant to human existence, to people young and old, their disturbances and difficulties and to the problems of society' (1991: 251). He further called for psychiatrists to be medically and sociologically 'valid, and to enable the mental health services to be responsive, lively, personal, and democratic in spirit' (1991: 251). Bourne had strong sentiments about the need to 're-professionalize' the psychiatrist in Britain and to counter the seeming irrelevance of psychiatry to everyday human affairs and concerns. Some of his students were aware of this apparent irrelevance when they commented that, based on their experience in various psychiatric settings, psychiatry amounted to administering two kinds of pill – tranquillizers and anti-depressants. Echoing this idea, Pilgrim has described psychiatrists as 'chemotherapists with a prescription pad' (2002: 591) and has foregrounded inclusive knowledge production.

Greater inclusion in knowledge production presupposes a position that takes into account all perspectives and all narrative accounts. The rise of the consumer movement in the latter part of the twentieth century has served to place consumers' voices and their narratives firmly on the mental health agenda. Although the consumer movement is a relatively new phenomenon, voices of protest and dissent have been raised and noted throughout history. An early recorded example of collective protest was 'the Petition of the Poor Distracted People in the House of Beldam' in 1620 (Campbell, 1996). A lobbying and campaigning organization called the Alleged Lunatics' Friends Society was formed in 1845 by 'ex-patients' and is credited with helping release the poet John Clare from a Victorian asylum. This is possibly one of the first examples of peer advocacy (Lester and Glasby, 2006). Over the years, the occasional consumer voice has been heard in terms of their individual experience and treatment in asylums and institutions. Porter quotes an early example of this in the individual narrative of John Percival. In 1838, Perceval published, 'A narrative of the treatment experienced by a gentleman during a state of mental derangement: Designed to explain the causes and the nature of insanity and to expose the injudicious conduct pursued towards many unfortunate sufferers under that calamity' (Porter, 1999: 182). Since that time, many consumers have written accounts of their experiences and many of these have become best-sellers. These include such books as those referred to earlier – Janet Frame's *An Angel at My Table* (2008), Susanna Kaysen's *Girl, Interrupted* (2000) and Kate Millett's *Flying* (1974).

Diagnosis and professional power

According to Porter, the history of madness is the history of power. He quotes a patient in a Parisian asylum early in the nineteenth century who is supposed to have cried out: 'I am man, God, Napoleon, Robespierre, altogether. I am Robespierre, a Monster. I must be slain' (Porter, 1987: 39). Porter continues by claiming, 'Because it imagines power, madness is both impotence and omnipotence'. In terms of possible claims to omnipotence, madness has been seen to require control. Power and authority in mental health care are associated with the act, and the consequences of diagnosis and of naming the set of signs and symptoms as an entity in itself'. According to Boyle, 'Diagnosis is central to the practice of psychiatry and receiving a psychiatric diagnosis can have a profound impact on people's lives' (2000: 69). Boyle questions the 'unarticulated assumptions' (2000: 76) about how people should act and their experiences and the emphasis placed in the Diagnostic and Statistical Manuals of Mental Disorders on an implied scientific rationality. She believes that it is questionable to treat the assumptions that underpin much of psychiatric diagnostic practice as if they were natural and immutable facts. Using Foucault's theory of the relationship between language, knowledge and power, she uncovers 'bio-power', the power of minds and bodies that resides in psychiatric diagnosis.

Following Foucault's (1977, 1980a) perspective, the disciplinary power of psychiatric diagnosis is manifested in three major ways. The first is the privileged way of talking about the signs and symptoms of people's mental distress and the assumption of the mantle of the expert. According to Barker, privileged language '…represents one of the simplest, yet potent, power tactics' (2000: 3). The combination of knowledge and power creates a pervasive barrier between the 'expert' and the 'patient' with the experiential knowledge or lived experience of the latter being downgraded.

The combination of language and power is associated with the second way in which the psychiatric diagnosis is imbued with authority. Language has the power to fix positions. When words such as 'delusions' or 'anxiety' are used to describe certain states, then this acts to create a reality in which the delusions and the anxiety exist. Furthermore, by using medical terminology, the impression is conveyed that there is '...inability of some internal mechanism to perform its natural functions' (Wakefield, 1992: 384). So, professional power is reinforced by the creation of a reality congruent with the psychiatric paradigm.

The third way in which professional power and knowledge is exercised is through the categorization of patients. Over the years, this disciplinary power has increased as new psychiatric diagnoses are discovered and new types of categories and persons are produced. This productivity can be seen in the ever-expanding World Health Organization's (WHO) International Classification of Disease (ICD) and the *American Psychiatric Association's Diagnostic and Statistical Manual of Mental Disorders* (DSM). In 1917, The American Psychiatric Association recognized 59 psychiatric disorders and with the introduction of the diagnostic and statistical manual (DSM) in 1952, this rose to 128 (Lester and Glasby, 2006). By 1980, with the publication of DSM-III, 227 categories were identified and in the 2000 edition of DSM-IV, 374 categories were listed (Biering, 2002; Lester and Glasby, 2006).

It is interesting to note that the American Psychiatric Association has attempted to accommodate difference and diversity by incorporating culture-specific disorders into its DSM framework (Prince and Tcheng-Larouche, 1987). However, despite vigorous debates around this incorporation, DSM-IV simply lists 'culture-bound syndromes' in an appendix. This lack of critical interrogation, which includes a lack of acknowledgement of power imbalances and charges of racism, can be seen to have continued in the ICD-10 (World Health Organization, 1993). This document merely lists, in an annexe to its criteria for research, a number of 'culture-specific disorders' drawn up by an anthropologist (Fernando, 2002).

The DSM-V (2013), continues to add to the overall range of diagnostic criteria. Lewis (2006) argues strongly from what he posits to be a postpsychiatry perspective, to 'decode' the DSM and expose it not as 'bad science' but as another form of rhetoric. For Lewis, the fact versus value distinction is a rhetorical move, designed to elevate and confirm scientific thinking as objective, value-neutral and true. Lewis rejects the long-hallowed distinction between rhetoric and logic, arguing instead that logical analyses are another form of rhetoric.

Fernando (2002) comments that although the terms used to diagnose mental states framed as illnesses have been realigned over the years and updated periodically, no amount of adaptation to changing needs alters the fundamental conceptual framework. In essence, he maintains that this leaves the frameworks themselves as culturally loaded and often racially biased with classification systems continuing to be founded on the philosophical basis of Western culture, reflecting 'the ethos of Western ideologies' (2002: 88). Nevertheless, Fernando (2002) tells us that the promise of the nosology of psychiatry being opened up to new ideas remains, even if its basic ethos stays constant.

In Foucault's view (1980b), this productive nature of psychiatry and the resulting disciplinary power of medicine differentiate it from the power of the law, which operates through prohibition and punishment. Boyle (2000) points out that in mental health legislation, juridical and disciplinary power join to create a situation in which there is power to subtract, to sanction, to prohibit or to impose upon people and their experiences, influencing in turn their rights and their future.

The importance of individual experiences, voices, individual narratives, and the contexts in which these are told, are increasingly being regarded as vital ingredients in the contested arena of mental health perspectives. Writing about his personal experience, a well-known 'survivor' of mental health services, Rob Coleman, says, 'Fourteen years ago, I was diagnosed as a schizophrenic, five years ago that was changed to chronic schizophrenia; three years ago I gave that up and went back to being Ron Coleman' (2000: 59). Coleman challenges the scientific nature of psychiatry by pointing out that individual psychiatrists differ in their diagnostic judgement and in his words, 'You go to see three different psychiatrists with the same symptoms and the chances are you'll get three different diagnoses depending on what the psychiatrists last read' (2000: 65).

Echoing the theme that it is the experience of mental distress and what people say about that experience that is paramount in our understanding, Marius Romme, Professor of Social

Psychiatry at the University of Maastricht in the Netherlands, has worked towards providing a demedicalized account of 'hearing voices' – the voice experience of many consumers. Romme's book, *Accepting Voices*, published in 1993, for both people who know the experience of hearing voices as well as for professionals, has been translated into six languages. His work with Sandra Escher, a journalist, has challenged the notion of individual psychopathology in psychiatry. Together, they have created the opportunity for understanding the voice experience as part of the human repertoire. They have offered an understanding that voices are not arbitrary, rather they carry significance in terms of the life story of the individual. Their work has paved the way for a different way of providing support. The Hearing Voices Network, built on the work of Romme and Escher, encourages positive working practices with people who hear voices and works to promote greater tolerance and understanding of voice hearing (http://www.hearing-voices.org). This network has over 40 groups across England, Scotland and Wales and is starting to have a presence in Australia. It offers voice hearers the opportunity to share their experiences using non-medical frameworks, and as a consequence validates voice hearers' experiences, making it possible for such experiences to become meaningful (Bracken and Thomas, 2001). Coleman (2002) has critiqued the diagnosis of hearing voices as a first-rank symptom of schizophrenia, arguing that the DSM-IV (*and V*) listings are limited. Going beyond noting the form the voices take, that is, whether the voices speak in the first, second or third person, Coleman argues that 'The content of the voices is regarded as being of no consequence; voices are seen as meaningless and without value' (2002: 151). Yet studies have found that there is a link between life events and the onset of voices (Ensink and Sauer, 1993; Romme and Escher, 1993). Coleman argues strongly for listening to the consumer's voice and exploring the link between trauma and ongoing distressing voices (2002).

By engaging in a human and connected way with the voice hearers, Romme and Escher have highlighted that validating consumers' experiences is not only eminently worthwhile but is also practical and ethical. Focusing on the idea that it is the narrative of the consumer that matters, consumer involvement is steadily gaining momentum in many countries. Consumers provide an invaluable resource. Borrill (2000) and Fawcett and

Karban (2005) point out that by recognizing the expertise of consumers – the fact that they are experts in what is happening to them – and learning from their in-depth knowledge, innovative partnerships can be forged within the context of support networks and service delivery.

It is also clear that from within the profession, psychiatrists are speaking out and calling for a new way of interpreting the experience of mental illness and listening to the voices of consumers (Bracken and Thomas, 2005; Lewis 2006). Bradley E. Lewis in *Moving Beyond Prozac, DSM and the New Psychiatry* (2006) argues that understandings of mental illness can never be undistorted by human interests. He posits that the paradigm shift in psychiatry away from eclectic approaches to mental distress towards neuroscience and the medical model constituted a political coup, orchestrated by powerful interests invested in making psychiatry fit mainstream medicine. Lewis forwards the notion that postpsychiatry strives for greater inclusion in knowledge production.

Concluding remarks

We will further develop the themes and arguments introduced in this chapter throughout this book, and we will appraise these across the lifespan in relation to children, young people, adults and older people. We will also explore the vistas and landscapes associated with 'dual diagnoses', families and 'caring'. Key areas for mental health practitioners will also be considered with these including anti-oppressive and anti-discriminatory practice, critical reflection, spatial analysis and social entrepreneurship. As part of this process, in Chapter 3 we turn to legal and ethical dilemmas in mental health and consider both the safeguards and the constraints of legislation in this complicated arena. However, to conclude this chapter, we draw from Bracken and Thomas (2005) and recognize that proposals and counter-proposals about madness and psychiatry have a long and colourful presence within the grand narrative of the history of madness. These serve not only to provide us with a richness in theoretical progression but also to offer us an opportunity to adopt a critical stance with regard to these theories and frameworks and their accompanying certainties.

CHAPTER 3

Legal and Ethical Dilemmas in Mental Health

It is clear that mental health legislation differs from nation to nation and in the United Kingdom, as well as in Australia, from country to country and from state to state. In Western nations particularly, mental health legislation is underpinned by psychiatric definitions and by medicalized frames of reference. As a result, terms such as 'mental disorder' and 'mental illness' predominate and tend to be uncritically utilized within the laws relating to mental health. It is also significant that mental health legislation has always been one of the most controversial areas of the law. As a result responses range from those who regard it as a means of safeguarding those who are vulnerable and out of control, to those who critique it for being overly paternalistic, for operating in a discriminatory and oppressive manner and for eroding basic human rights. Whatever the perspective taken, mental health legislation plays a pivotal role in the complex arena of mental health and mediates between the state and the individual, with considerations relating to the protection of both featuring significantly. It also provides the overarching framework for the provision of services, and although dealing particularly with involuntary admission and treatment, it can also provide the means for ensuring that minimum standards are maintained in both hospital and community settings.

In this chapter, we explore the underlying rationales for mental health legislation and appraise issues relating to implementation. We also examine the general principles and underlying value systems which govern responses to those diagnosed as experiencing mental disorder and unpack what has become the almost sloganized refrain of 'evidence-based practice'. Terminology is always important, and we need to point out that in this chapter we use the terms found in mental health legislation. It does need to be noted, however, that for purposes of brevity, and not withstanding some differentiation in some legislative contexts, we refer to both 'mental disorder' and 'mental illness' as 'mental disorder'. In this, we appreciate that this term also reflects the changes introduced by The Mental Health Act (2007) in England and Wales where 'mental disorder' now refers generally to 'any disorder of the mind or brain'.

The rationales for mental health legislation

Mental health legislation has historically been driven by the concept of managing risk for the purpose of providing safety for all. This can in part be attributed to the unfounded linking of mental disorder with violence. In this, it has to be pointed out that acts of violence and/or harm perpetrated by individuals with a diagnosed mental disorder are relatively small. Fawcett and Karban (2005), drawing on the available statistics, highlight that only a very small proportion of the homicides of strangers can be linked to individuals with a previous history of mental disorder. Available statistics in Australia also show that 90 per cent of people with a diagnosed mental illness have no history of violence and that most acts of violence are carried out by people without a history of mental disorder (Mindframe, 2010). However, perceived threats of violence remain a dominating factor and perhaps explain the greater rates of involuntary detention for some groups rather than others. In England and Wales, for example, it has long been accepted that racist constructions affect the ways in which young African-Caribbean men disproportionately feature in the statistics for compulsory detention (DOH, 2003; Fernando, 2003; SCMH, 2006), and this area is explored in greater detail in Chapter 6. In Australia, it has also long been the case that Indigenous Australians are three to five times more likely to be admitted to psychiatric facilities on an involuntary basis than non-Indigenous Australians (Mindframe, 2010).

Prevailing legislation in Western nations attempts to manage the dichotomy of protecting individuals diagnosed as experiencing a mental disorder whilst also protecting those around them. Notions of rights also feature and mental health legislation defines those rights available to individuals subject to compulsory detention. Whilst the specifying of basic rights to those who have had the right to liberty taken away from them may appear somewhat contradictory, countries and states are obliged to pay attention to international human rights legislation in the drafting of mental health laws. However, it does need to be noted that whilst not all countries have mental health legislation, of those countries that do, the World Health Organization (WHO, 2003, 2009) reports that only half have legislation which has been passed since 1990. This means that some countries continue to apply legislation which to varying extents contravenes recent human rights declarations. The WHO (2003, 2009) argues that it is essential that countries establish legislative review programmes and amend their legislation in line with contemporary research findings and prevailing cultural contexts. As part of this process, the WHO (2003, 2009) specifically recommends that the scope of legislative reform be extended from its historical focus on hospitalization and argues that community integration should be addressed. Within this, they strongly recommend the involvement of all relevant stakeholders. This, they make clear includes those diagnosed as having mental disorders as well as professional groups. The WHO (2003, 2009) maintains that the needs and rights of 'carers' in particular should be balanced with the needs and rights of individuals and that these considerations need to be included in legislative reform to ensure a more holistic approach to mental health service delivery.

Mental health legislation – issues of implementation

The mental health legislation which operates throughout Australia, Scotland, Northern Ireland, England and Wales is charged with addressing a number of competing issues. These include paying attention to the rights, dignity and self-respect of individuals, focusing on the least restrictive option and protecting the public from possible harm. Practitioners also have to act in accordance with their codes of professional ethics. This latter requirement can lead to inconsistencies, as different mental health professionals subscribe to different codes of professional ethics. It can also generate tensions between a practitioner's legal duty and their particular professional ethical code. This can be seen in relation to social workers who (as approved mental health professionals in England and Wales under The Mental Health Act, 2007, and as approved mental health practitioners with regard to the mental health legislation in force in the states and territories in Australia[1]) have to juggle the requirements of their professional code of ethics, which emphasizes the importance of promoting autonomy and self-determination, with their obligations under predominantly paternalistic mental health legislation. As Banks (2006) points out, the law tells us that if we make the technical (and ethical) judgement that the disorder is such that it is in the patient's interest to be detained in hospital, then we have the powers to do this, but the law does not tell us what we *ought* to do, just what we *can* do.

Applying concepts of rights, as highlighted, can also be far from straightforward for mental health professionals. As we have already seen, there can be disparity between national and international understandings of human rights and between the rights of the individual and the rights of the general public. However, in relation to basic legal rights, Ellis-Jones (2002) draws attention to the 'hearing rule'. He argues that it is an essential rule of general law that a person is informed of the case to be made against them and that they are given the opportunity of replying to it before any decision is made that would deprive them of their rights and/or civil liberties. This rule is clearly disregarded when involuntary admission is being considered as this usually occurs at a time of crisis. Nevertheless, an assessment that an individual is deemed to be a risk either to themselves or to others places them at a legal disadvantage. The compromise effected by Ellis Jones (2002) is generally regarded as reflecting good practice, in that whilst acknowledging the extent of the legal disparity and accepting that an individual may be in considerable mental distress, it maintains that at the very minimum an individual needs to receive clear and sensitively framed information, given verbally and in writing, about what is happening to them, what to expect and what their legal rights are. This point is echoed by La

---

[1] It needs to be noted that the terminology used can vary between the six states and three territories in Australia.

Fond and Srebnik (1999) who maintain that virtually everyone involved in the commitment process would prefer a voluntary solution. They acknowledge the difficult role that approved mental health professionals have to play, but highlight the importance of practitioners operating with sensitivity and respect, paying full attention to ensuring that the rights of the person compulsorily detained are communicated in written as well as in verbal forms and that these rights are clearly adhered to.

Practitioners in the mental health field are increasingly charged with assessing, on the basis of medical history and current circumstances, the 'risk' posed by an individual to themselves and others and with managing this 'risk' over time. As Fawcett et al. (2010) point out, risk management in policy and practice documentation is often presented in a very straightforward manner. Risk assessments are seen as being able to identify 'at risk' individuals, to assign probable 'risk' trajectories and, via a process of 'risk management', to ensure primarily that medication is taken and that an optimum level of functioning is attained. Critiques of 'risk' assessment and risk management focus on risk assessments predominately associating risk with danger and, as a consequence, serving to negate the positive aspects of risk taking for all individuals. The assumed externally quantifiable nature of 'risk' and the belief that it is possible to apply a form of cost-benefit analysis to human behaviour have also been persistently challenged and accompanying charges of reductionism have been levied (Heyman, 1998). In a similar vein, the implications of the incorporation of unacknowledged value judgements and cultural preferences into risk assessment procedures and practices have been highlighted (Fawcett, 2009). Fawcett (2000a) asserts that the manner in which risks are viewed, the weighting attached to certain consequences, the influence of prevailing cultural and social values, the importance of specific contexts and contextual considerations, and the ways in which these factors throw doubt on the efficacy and veracity of straightforward rational judgements about risk, make risk assessment and management a far more complicated process than is often assumed (Fawcett, 2000a: 32).

The concept of risk and the place currently afforded to risk assessment and risk management processes are areas we return to frequently throughout this book. However, at this point, in relation to legislative and policy frameworks, we do want to particularly draw attention to the discrepancy between objectively presented assumptions of what is possible and the uncertainty that surrounds assessments of probability in practice.

Continuing with the theme of mental health legislation implementation, we now turn our attention towards the considerable powers vested in approved mental health professionals and practitioners by means of the mental health laws. Although, as highlighted in this chapter, the various Mental Health Acts, operating in both the United Kingdom and Australia, generally require an individual to be given appropriate treatment in the least restrictive environment, with interference to rights, dignity and self-respect (taking account of the prevailing circumstances) being kept to a minimum, clear power imbalances do provide challenges. Similarly, complexities exist in policy climates which promote the 'empowerment' of mental health service users and consumers whilst simultaneously prioritizing the 'expert' knowledge of mental health professionals and practitioners over experiential knowledge or lived experience. Rees (1991: 17) draws from Foucault to state that 'the appropriate way to understand power is to focus not on the mechanics of control exercised by central or sovereign authorities, but on the experiences of the subjects of such control'. Foucault (1980a, 1980b, 1981) conceptualizes power not as a fixed phenomenon which some people possess and others do not, but rather as a force which continually circulates through net-like organizations where individuals can both be subject to the effects of power as well as be the vehicles for its articulation. In terms of the enactment of legislation and the operation of power dynamics, this can be seen to direct attention not only towards how legislative powers are exercised but also to those with experiential knowledge of the effects. Accordingly it can be argued, and this is a position we fully support, that it is only by foregrounding the experiences of those subject to compulsory detention that the considerable power imbalances that exist between mental health professionals and practitioners and compulsorily detained individuals can start to be ameliorated.

Controversy surrounding community treatment orders and hospital treatment

In most of Australia, as well as in the United Kingdom generally, mental health legislation has been subject to recent review and change. The reasons for this include a perceived need to alter the balance between legal and medical responsibilities and powers, the need to reflect changes in international human rights legislation, the influence of pressure groups representing 'carers' and service users or consumers, the need to take account of the ongoing effects of deinstitutionalization and community care policies and, associated with this, the drive for treatment to take place in 'the least restrictive setting'. With regard to this latter area, Community Treatment Orders (CTOs) have assumed a position of particular importance. In Australia, for example, CTOs have been brought in at different times and have taken particular forms as the six individual states and two territories have enacted separate mental health legislation. The following is a breakdown of all the states and territories and the date of their current mental health legislation:

- New South Wales: Mental Health Act 2007
- Victoria: Mental Health Act 1986
- Queensland: Mental Health Act 2000, Mental Health Regulation 2002
- Western Australia: Mental Health Act 1996
- Tasmania: Mental Health Act 1996
- South Australia: Mental Health Act 2010
- Northern Territory: Mental Health Act 1998
- Australian Capital Territory: Mental Health (Treatment and Care) Act 1994

In the United Kingdom, a similar breakdown is as follows:

- England and Wales, 2007
- Scotland, 2003
- Northern Ireland, 1986 (currently subject to the Bamford Review)

It is notable that although CTOs have been incorporated into the legislation in the states and territories in Australia, as well as in Canada and New Zealand for some years, it was only with the review and amendment of The Mental Health Act (1983) in 2007 and its replacement by The Mental Health Act (2007) that, amid great controversy, the provision for CTOs was enacted in England and Wales. Unlike Australia, Canada and New Zealand, rather than being, rather uncontroversially, regarded as a means of further supporting policies of deinstitutionalization and 'care in the community', the introduction of CTOs in England and Wales was predominantly regarded as invasive and as a further erosion of individual liberties and human rights. The place of CTOs in the 2007 Mental Health Act in England and Wales remains contested, and although it is still too early to assess the overall effect of its introduction, it is interesting to review the situation in Scotland. Lawton-Smith (2006) looked at the use being made of CTOs in Scotland 18 months after implementation. He found that despite the 'new' Scottish legislation being criticized as being difficult to understand and concerns being expressed about ethical issues and civil liberties, the use of the CTOs increased over time. It is also notable that this increase occurred in the face of stated opposition from mental health professionals, who made it clear that it was not their role to 'act as police', and in the light of limited understanding by professionals, consumers and carers of the extent of CTO powers. Lawton-Smith (2006) draws attention to the growth in the use of CTOs taking place against a backdrop of reduced resources, with additional funding not being made available to support the introduction and implementation of this provision. The Scottish example can be used to highlight that, notwithstanding the difference posed by Banks (2006) and referred to earlier between 'ought' and 'can', once a power is available, its use appears to become inevitable.

The above discussion clearly draws attention to the different ways in which provisions such as CTOs have been both viewed and utilized. Accepting that CTOs have their critics in Australia, Canada and New Zealand, the majority view appears to be that they constitute a means of furthering deinstitutionalizing treatment programmes and promoting community-orientated, less restrictive options than compulsory detention in hospital. However, the controversy surrounding the introduction of this provision in England and Wales, as well as in Scotland, highlights that for others CTOs are regarded as further extensions of the ever increasing powers of mental health legislation and of the continued prevailing dominance of clinically orientated mental health discourses and treatment regimes (Lewis, 2009).

Another area of continuing debate in relation to current mental health legislation in Western nations relates to the ongoing provision of hospital beds. As highlighted in Chapter 1, the extent to which deinstitutionalization policies were meant to increase or reduce beds in psychiatric wards in general hospitals was never clearly resolved, and the ongoing shortage of resources for community care has kept this issue on the agenda. The Australian situation serves as a good example of how events have unfolded. Here, the Richmond Report (1982), a well pro-moted and highly influential document, operated as a catalyst for change when it recommended that individuals diagnosed with mental health disorders should be moved out of mental health inpatient facilities/hospitals and integrated back into the community. However, the Report, whilst making this recommen-dation, also stated that hospital services would continue to be essential for providing acute and long-term mental health care for some individuals. This part of the Report however failed to gain sufficient traction. The result, over recent decades has been for 'deinstitutionalization' and 'community care' to become buzz words which have been used in economic and policy terms to justify a reduction in the overall availability of hospital beds throughout Australia without attention being paid to appropri-ately funding or supporting community-based forms of support.

These events can be seen to have been mirrored in other Western nations, fuelling, as highlighted, the ongoing debate about the number of hospital beds required. In terms of future policy directions, there are those who argue that the continued provision of hospital beds is essential to ensure that a range of responses remain available. However, there are others who main-tain that community care has been significantly underfunded and that an appropriate response is not to provide more hospital beds, but to realistically fund user-led community care support systems (Golightley, 2008). There are also, clearly, a range of positions in between.

Notwithstanding the varying arguments put forward, it is clear that a reduction in mental health hospital beds aligned with an underfunding of community care options has exacerbated system pressures. As a result, a trend is emerging where indi-viduals experiencing mental distress are having to attend general hospital emergency departments. Research by Stefan (2006) indi-cates that emergency departments of general hospitals in the United States are overwhelmed by an increasing number of mental health consumers. He argues that utilizing these general health resources not only reduces the number of emergency beds available for those with physical complaints but is also inappropriate. Further to this, Stefan (2006) maintains that emergency department staff are increasingly becoming involved in providing crisis care and implementing mental health legislation. Work by Samuels (2008) found that in the four countries that comprise the United Kingdom, mental health consumers presenting to emergency departments are often met with a 'patchy and 'ad hoc service' as emergency department staff have not the facilities to respond appropriately and are not trained to work in the mental health field. The State Government of Victoria (2008) in Australia has also recognized that general hospital emergency departments have become a key point of contact within the health system for individuals experiencing mental health crises. As a result, Victorian policy directives (2008) point to the need to improve emergency care processes to reduce delays in mental health assessments, to grant access to mental health hospital beds if required, to greatly improve discharge planning and to increase access to community support services. In England and Wales, the Disability Rights Commission (2007) has clearly recognized the effects of resource constraints, but has chosen to foreground issues of equality, rights, citizenship and choice. As a result, they place primary emphasis not on 'top-down' policy planning, but on 'people with mental health conditions'[2] determining the range of services and responses that would work for them.

Despite clear resource constraints and diverging responses to increased calls for inclusivity and service user representation in mental health service planning forums, the concepts of deinstitutionalization and 'community care' continue to inform mental health policy and legislative frames in countries such as Australia, the United Kingdom, Canada, the United States and New Zealand. However, Marusic and Brecelj (2000) highlight the difficulties facing those countries where policies relating to community mental health care have not yet been developed. They cite Slovenia, as an example of a country which, despite having undergone significant political, social and economic change in the past ten years, due to a lack of funding has still not been in a position to develop a clear plan for the integration and the implementation of community mental health services. Jenkins (2005)

---

[2] This is the term used throughout this Report.

identifies countries such as Georgia, Bulgaria and Lithuania as having developed comprehensive strategies for improving mental health services and in particular for preventing suicide, but reports that the implementation of such strategies is limited due to financial restraints. Restricted financial resources in these countries have resulted in a limited capacity to implement change, and they largely continue to use institutionalization, as they have done historically, as a means of managing individuals who have been diagnosed with mental disorders.

Although countries such as Australia, the United Kingdom, Canada, the United States and New Zealand are seen as being at the forefront of legislative reform in relation to mental health, Glaves (2006) points out that despite a general lack of specifically funded community mental health services, the recovery rate in countries such as South America and Africa is twice as high as it is in the West. Glaves argues that this is because, in non-Western countries, the behaviour that causes people to be diagnosed with mental disorders is seen in spiritual terms or as a reaction to trauma or a personal crisis. As a result, instead of medicalized treatment patterns, the individual is largely supported by their family and their local community. Although this response clearly places pressure on families and communities and highlights resource constraints, it also draws attention to the prevailing significance of cultural and social differences with regard to understandings as well as experiences of mental distress. It further serves to emphasize the importance of paying attention to and understanding an individual's personal narrative within their prevailing social, cultural and economic context.

Recent legislative change affecting the role of 'carers'

Whilst issues relating to the notion of 'caring' and the role of 'carers' are considered in detail in Chapter 9, at this point it is useful to review the increasing attention paid to 'carers' in recent legislation. This can be seen to reflect both the increasing acknowledgement by governments of the contribution made by 'carers' in assisting recovery and also the understanding that support for 'carers' decreases the economic demands made on mental health systems generally. We will therefore look both at the changing recognition of 'carers' in legislation and policy and also at the implications of this for both service users and 'carers'.

The changing recognition of 'carers' can be illustrated by referring to the Australian context and to two pieces of significant legislation in New South Wales – The Mental Health Act, 1990, and The Mental Health Act, 2007. It is notable that the 1990 legislation addressed the rights of 'carers' in a very minimalist manner with only limited provision being made available for close relatives of a compulsorily detained individual to access information about their condition and treatment. In contrast, the Mental Health Act, 2007, introduced the concept of 'primary carer'. This enables and requires a 'patient' to nominate a person to have the right to information about their condition and treatment plan and to be involved in discharge planning. It is notable that the appointment of a 'primary carer' can take place at any time and applies both to involuntary treatment in hospital as well as in the community.

In Australia, generally, the importance of involving 'carers' was recognized in policy terms as long ago as 1996 when The National Standards for Mental Health Services were produced (Commonwealth Department of Health and Ageing, 1996). As discussed elsewhere, these standards underpin The National Practice Standards for the Mental Health Workforce (2002) (Commonwealth Department of Health and Ageing, 2002). The National Standards for Mental Health Services (Commonwealth Department of Health and Ageing, 1996) and the Revised National Standards for Mental Health Services (Commonwealth Department of Health and Ageing, 2010) emphasize that:

- There is a current individual care plan for each individual, which is constructed and regularly reviewed with the individual and, with the individual's informed consent, their carers and that this plan is available to them and may involve the participation of other persons nominated by the individual, such as their advocate, general practitioner, private psychiatrist and other service providers.
- Each individual receives assistance to develop a plan which identifies early warning signs of recurring difficulties and appropriate action and that carers are involved with the individual's free and informed consent.

• Individuals must give informed consent before their personal information is communicated to health professionals outside the mental health service, to carers or other agencies or people.

As pointed out in the Mental Health Council of Australia's 'Not for Service' Report produced in 2005, territories and states have struggled to implement these standards. However, the ratification in policy does ensure that responsibilities are clear and that resource and system constraints remain on the national agenda.

In England and Wales, the 1989 White Paper produced by Sir Roy Griffiths entitled 'Caring for People' (DOH, 1989) ensured that the role of 'carers' was acknowledged with support being enshrined in the subsequent National Health Services and Community Care Act (1990). The Carers (Recognition and Services) Act 1995 further recognized 'carers' roles and responsibilities and put in place building blocks for future development. Although this Act was criticized for paying insufficient attention to resource issues, it did serve to firmly place 'carers' within the legislative framework and to raise the profile of the 'carers' agenda generally. The Mental Health Policy Implementation Guide: Support, Time and Recovery (STR) Workers, issued in 2003, can also be seen to be important as it significantly extended the role of 'carers', as well as consumers, beyond family settings. In this context, this policy document not only refers to 'carers' and consumers as active participants in service development and evaluation, but also pays attention to how they can be employed as members of mental health teams.

However, although, the recognition in legislation in countries such as Australia (NSW) and England and Wales of the role played by informal 'carers' gives formal recognition to a group formerly characterized by their invisibility, there can be seen to be mixed implications for service users and 'carers' in the arena of mental health. As highlighted, we explore these matters more fully in Chapter 9, but at this stage it is important to draw attention to the possible tensions between an individual's right to privacy and autonomy and to the power imbalances which can ensue as a result of the designation of roles such as 'carer' and, by implication, 'the cared for'. Although legislation is increasingly incorporating the 'patient's' views as to who the 'primary carer' should be (The Mental Health Act, NSW, 2007), and there is increasing flexibility about the inclusion of civil partners, with the displacement of the legally designated 'nearest relative' on the grounds of unsuitability being on the statues (The Mental Health Act, 2007, England and Wales), these issues remain pertinent. The Mental Health Act (2007) in NSW, Australia, for example, highlights some of these tensions as it is only at the time that an initial assessment is made in the community, prior to a decision being made to mandate treatment, that an individual's right to full privacy and confidentiality cannot be overridden by the rights of 'carers' to information about their relative's treatment status and plan. The possible conflict of interest brought about by this well-intentioned legislative change (which is clearly reflected in legislation elsewhere) can easily result in the views of family members or 'carers' being prioritized over those of individuals diagnosed with a mental disorder. Another consideration is highlighted by Mickel (2008) in the context of the legislative changes relating to 'carers' brought in by The Mental Health Act (2007) in England and Wales. On the one hand, family 'carers' are now to be consulted and included in the formulation of care plans, however, on the other hand, they are placed in a position where they may be expected to act as wardens reporting to service providers about their relatives. This has the potential to not only adversely affect family relationships but also to place additional expectations and responsibilities upon family members who take on the roles of 'carers'.

Advance directives

Advance directives are a relatively new concept in the area of mental health and for many can be seen as a means of redressing some of the power imbalances embedded in mental health legislation. Originally, advance directives were introduced for 'end-of-life' medical decisions, and they are intended to determine an individual's treatment preferences. Advance directives have been promoted by mental health service user campaigning groups, such as MIND in the United Kingdom, as a means of service users maintaining control over what happens to them when involuntary detention and/or treatment becomes an option. Hanlon and Taylor (2002), who as authors represent a consumer and service provider partnership, describe advance directives as an empowering tool which can promote a more holistic approach to mental health within clinical discourses through:

- Promoting independence and responsibility in the maintenance of their own health status.
- Providing opportunities for individuals to identify relevant people in their recovery/treatment plan/advance directive.
- Respecting the privacy, rights and confidentiality of the individual by identifying people and their roles within their recovery plan/advance directive throughout the various phases.

However, advance directives in the arena of mental health continue to remain controversial. There has been criticism from some practitioners who maintain that there is a need for greater procedural guidance and clarity about how to initiate, implement and/or revoke these instruments (Srebnik and Kim, 2006). There is also a paradox, in that although the use of advance directives is fundamentally to reduce coercion by optimizing individual consultation and collaboration, an individual must be considered mentally competent in order to execute such a directive. However, despite wariness on the part of practitioners and the competency paradox, laws specifically authorizing mental health advance directives have been enacted in 12 states in the United States. Some of these laws (e.g. Alaska and Oregon) apply only to written declarations concerning inpatient mental health treatment, psychotropic medications and electroconvulsive therapy (ECT), whilst others apply to both inpatient and community mental health treatments. Although, there is much work to be done, it is apparent that advance directives can serve as a means of redressing the power imbalances embedded in current mental health legislation and recognizing the experiential knowledge of service users.

Evidence-based practice

Evidence-based practice is a term which has gained considerable currency in mental health services, and as in this book we highlight the importance of the experiential knowledge of service users and consumers, it is useful to explore this area in greater detail at this point.

In medical and indeed in government settings, evidence-based practice is often taken to mean the findings produced by means of randomized controlled trials. These for a long time have been regarded as the 'gold standard' of research methodologies. However, as we see in Chapter 4, when research using this methodology is unpacked, the situation is not as clear cut as it first appears. In particular 'objectivity' can be uncloaked, and once the wrappings of non-interrogated values and assumptions are taken away, this concept can be revealed as yet another form of subjectivity. As such it retains considerable value, but of necessity loses its ascribed pre-eminent dominance. This 'uncloaking' also expands the research canvas so that 'evidence' from positivistic quantitative projects can share the frame with qualitative research undertakings. These can include research approaches such as Participant Action Research, which as the name suggests fully involves participants in research projects, not as research subjects, but as research partners. The expanding of the canvas also serves to emphasize the importance of mixed-method approaches to research and the benefits of not restricting 'evidence' to narrow and rigid parameters. Research clearly needs to be carried out in a rigorous, transparent and reflexive manner, but we maintain that to be seen as 'evidence', it should not have to pass through the eye of a positivist needle.

Trish Greenhalgh, who has operated as Professor of Primary Health Care at the Royal Free Hospital and University College, London, and as Director of the Unit for Evidence-Based Practice and Policy, has maintained that there is no paradox in upholding individual narrative and respecting the interpreted story of clients with the generalized information that comes from population-derived evidence. She has written, '...the truths established by the empirical observation of populations in randomized trials and cohort studies, cannot be mechanistically applied to individual patients or episodes of illness, whose behaviour is irremediably contextual and (seemingly) idiosyncratic' (1998: 251). Consequently, she makes connections between opposing stances and highlights that narrative interpretivist approaches produce 'evidence' and that mixed-method approaches have much to recommend them.

The making of links between different perspectives, research approaches and diverse forms of 'evidence' can be seen to be gathering momentum and to be creating what Bracken and

Thomas refer to as '...a new deal between health professionals and service users' (2001: 724). Muir Gray (1999) in a call
for 'postmodern health', where there is acknowledgement of a
variety of forms of knowledge and a non-prioritization of 'expert
knowledge', believes that overall there is a renewed concern for
greater links to be made between values and evidence, risks and
benefits with consumer involvement and participation playing
a central and pivotal role. Within this, it also has to be recognized that the views and experiences of consumers/service users
are heterogeneous and often conflicting. However, the acknowledgement of difference and complexity serves to paint a much
more detailed picture which enriches rather than reduces interaction. In terms of the involvement of mental health professionals
in this process, as all those working in the arena of mental health
know, they are operating in environments where their experiential knowledge together with their capacity for critical analysis
and their ability to operate strategically have to be fully utilized.
In Chapter 10, we explore the differences between technocratic
and dynamic approaches; that is, the differences between a role
where mental health professionals implement set procedures in
a standardized manner and one where they innovate and direct,
and we highlight the negative consequences of the former model
for consumers and service users. Although mental health professionals are subject to many constraints, we feel that it is important
at this stage to emphasize the opportunities brought about by
interaction and participation and to draw attention to the many
forms that subjectification and exclusion can take.

It is also useful at this point to look at the political nature of
'evidence'. France and Utting (2005) and Stevens (2007) variously
maintain that overall there are too many competing interests
and agendas for policy and practice to be directly linked to
research. Fawcett et al. (2010), as part of their discussion of
this topic, look at how even those who hold a technocratic view
and believe that the power of science can rationally inform
policy making continually critique policy makers for prioritizing ideology and expediency over the 'best' evidence. However,
Fawcett et al. (2010) although questioning whether research can
ever directly affect policy do not go on to say that research
has no importance, relevance or impact, rather they argue that
although political factors influence how research is used, research
is important to:

- create climates for change, and this can be seen in relation to equal opportunities and anti-racist policies;
- break new ground, as in the example of Hearing Voices Networks; and
- appraise the effect of policies and practices *with* those charged with their delivery as well as with those who are meant to benefit from them.

Concluding remarks

Clearly, legal decision-making, which involves involuntary hospital admissions and/or treatment, contains a number of dilemmas. These relate to the interpretative nature of decision-making processes, the part played by clinical knowledge, the operation of power dynamics and values, as well as the influence of subjective understandings. Current legislative reform continues to have a strong clinical orientation and to privilege medical frames of reference. However, increasingly there is a move towards placing emphasis on a more holistic approach to mental health, on incorporating experiential understandings and to turning a critical but constructive lens towards legislation, policies and practices.

We will continue to explore these areas as we move on, in Chapters 4 and 5, to consider mental health issues across the lifespan, beginning with a focus on children and young people.

PART II

Mental Health across the Lifespan

CHAPTER 4

Children's Matters

As we turn to consider issues relating to children and mental health, it is clear that the promotion of good mental health in children and the prevention of mental ill-health are areas which are subscribed to by all. However, statistics show that mental ill-health is affecting younger and younger children on a worldwide basis, and it is notable that in the United Kingdom approximately 20 per cent of children are diagnosed as having a mental health condition in any given year (The Office for National Statistics, UK, 2005). In Australia, the figure is around 14 per cent (Mindframe, 2009). Mental ill-health in childhood is increasingly being linked to problems which manifest themselves in adolescence and also adulthood in terms of social exclusion. These are seen to include poor interpersonal relationships, self-harm, erratic employment patterns as well as offending behaviour. It has been estimated that the cost of responding to these areas is rising, and it has been suggested that the expenditure on public services used through to adulthood by individuals with troubled behaviour as children is ten times higher than the average (Social Exclusion Unit, UK, 2005; Fraser and Blishen, 2007; Australian Social Inclusion Board, 2010).

Many reasons have been given to explain the rise in the statistics. These range from more clinical attention being paid to diagnosing mental illness in children, to the number of stress-related factors both increasing and affecting larger numbers of younger children. There is also debate about the extent to which the figures represent a marked rise in the number of children actually experiencing mental ill-health or whether the situation is more complex and that more children, for a variety of reasons, are being seen or constructed as experiencing an expanding range of disorders. Clearly, there is much overlap between these explanatory frames, and the statistics reflect a range of influencing factors. In this chapter, we will explore some of the prevailing perspectives in greater detail and we will review the implications for children and families. As part of this process, particular attention will be paid to the marked increase in the diagnosis of conditions such as Attention Deficit Hyperactivity Disorder (ADHD).

The diagnosis of mental illness in children

Golightley (2008) points out that clinical problems relating to children under five are usually associated with communication difficulties, sleeping problems, unusually strong and frequently exhibited tantrums and long-lasting anxiety displayed after major traumas, such as the death of a parent. In children of school age who have not yet become adolescents, issues tend to relate to hyperactivity, bedwetting or soiling, poor relationships, challenging behaviours and matters associated with school attendance. Emphasis tends to be placed on managing the behaviours or symptoms, although clinical researchers such as Shonkoff (2005) make links between precipitants (such as extreme poverty, physical or emotional abuse, chronic neglect, severe maternal depression, substance abuse and family violence) and the production of toxic stress which, he maintains, disrupts brain architecture. Shonkoff (2005) argues that changes in the architecture of the developing brain impair stress management systems, thereby increasing the risk of stress-related physical and mental illnesses.

Although only a very small proportion of children are diagnosed as requiring specialist intervention, there can be variations of opinion relating to when clinical intervention is required. Aspects such as severity, duration and the extent of the disruption caused tend to feature significantly and diagnoses applied to children include depressive, hyperkinetic and dissociative disorders. Treatments can include forms of drug therapy, cognitive behaviour therapy, systemic and family therapy and various forms of counselling. There has been much discussion in recent years about the increasing medicalization of the social sphere (Skolbekken, 2008) and, given that in schools especially, additional resources can only be accessed if specific conditions are diagnosed, it can be argued that the increase in the number of clinical diagnoses may relate to more attention being paid to this area. However, as highlighted above, it is also claimed that children are subject to more pressures than ever before, and we will now go on to consider this area in greater detail.

Stress-related factors

The pressures which children now face are considerable, with factors such as body image, changing parental relationships, the pressure to achieve and the importance attached to maintaining credibility with peers featuring significantly. School experiences are of considerable importance, and bullying is increasingly being acknowledged as a major source of mental distress for children. Media campaigns, such as those focusing on childhood obesity, although well intentioned, can also serve to target those children who are already being adversely affected by strained relationships with peers. Although this chapter focuses particularly on children under 12, most definitions of children refer to those under 16. The Mission Australia Snapshots (2009a, 2011), which asked young Australians what concerned them most, showed that children and young people ranked drugs, suicide and body image as the top three issues, followed by family conflict, bullying/emotional abuse, alcohol, physical/sexual abuse, personal safety, coping with stress, depression, school or study problems, the environment, self-harm, discrimination and sexuality, with the latter focusing specifically on sexual relationships, health and identity. Just over half of those surveyed were in the 11–14-year-old age group, and although just over a quarter of all respondents ranked the top three items as areas of major concern, at least eight of these aspects were highlighted as being significant for at least one in five respondents.

Most children live in families or in family settings, and although family compositions vary enormously, approaches to parenting and parenting styles are clearly very influential. 'The 'Sure Start' initiative in England and Wales clearly focused on parents and children and fostered interagency collaboration with the aim of promoting a joined-up approach to parental and family support, early years education and health promotion. It operated across the departments of education, health, work and pensions, and as Featherstone (2004) outlines, its purpose was to enable families to access flexible child care, early learning and family and health support by means of a single point of contact. It comprised an important aspect of the Labour Government's emphasis on social investment and social inclusion and achieved significant results.

From a psychological perspective, parenting capacity and style are seen to affect emotional and cognitive development as well as levels of resilience (Stewart-Brown and Shaw, 2002). Key protective factors have been identified as feeling loved, trusted and understood, having a strong interest in life, having an optimistic outlook, being able to exercise autonomy and being able to demonstrate self-acceptance (Mental Health Foundation, 2007). Lone-parent families, together with reconstituted and large families, have long been regarded as incorporating additional risk factors for children in terms of their mental health. However, research findings have pointed out that possible risk factors are associated more with children's experiences of parenting capacity than with family structure per se (Mental Health Foundation, 2001, 2007). It is also notable that children in the care system, young carers, children of refugees and asylum seekers and children with intellectual disabilities, as a result of the additional pressures they face, are regarded as having a greater likelihood of experiencing mental distress (Mental Health Foundation, 2001).

There have also been studies looking at the characteristics of parents who drop out of early intervention programmes focusing on the mental health of their children. Those most likely to disengage have been reported as including younger parents, those in less stable relationships and those with lower levels of educational attainment (Murray, 2000). However, other studies have indicated that the way intervention is delivered, dissatisfaction with the forms of intervention on offer, problems with the accessibility of services and a perceived improvement in the identified problem area also influence the drop out rates from early intervention programmes (Cornah, 2002).

Entry to school constitutes a very important period for all children, and it is a time when children are most likely to experience difficult or fractured transitions. Fraser and Blishen (2007) highlight that schools have an important role to play in protecting and fostering good mental health and that in England emotional health has been promoted by means of the Healthy Schools Programme. Fraser and Blishen (2007) advocate 'whole school approaches' and comment that programmes that are limited to the classroom are less likely to be effective. They also note, in line with a Report produced by the National Association of Schoolmasters and Union of Women Teachers (2005), that when additional support is required, receiving help from a school-based rather than an external counselling service is perceived by pupils to be less stigmatizing. Parents who have previously refused referrals to external mental health specialists have also been found to be more likely to allow their children to see a school counsellor. In line with this finding, they highlight that when an in-school counsellor is available, teachers are more likely to refer pupils for help.

Within schools, anti-bullying strategies have been promoted as a key means of facilitating mental well-being and alleviating individual distress (Olweus, 1995; Mental Health Foundation, 2007). However, Fraser and Blishen (2007) additionally report that while teachers feel that there are many good initiatives available, there remains a need for greater resources, more consistent support for all schools and for innovative and creative thinking with regard to mental health promotion and mental ill-health prevention. In this, they regard head teachers as having a central role to play in developing positive mental health strategies within their schools.

When we look at areas that can negatively impact on a child's well-being and mental health overall, the various ways in which aspects relating to social class, gender, sexuality, ethnicity and geographical location intersect and impact on some children have to be taken into account (Coleman and Schofield, 2001). Green and Taylor (2010) look at the relationship between gender and child health in countries with both low and high economic resources. With regard to the former they point to gendered power relations and the frequent devaluing of girl children as opposed to boy children, subjecting many girl children to multiple levels of disadvantage. Tangible disadvantages, which have accompanying mental health components, include varying levels of malnutrition, the adverse effects of cultural practices such as female genital mutilation and the acceptability of early marriages and pregnancy. Less tangible effects brought about by pervasive gendered power imbalances include fewer educational and life course opportunities, fewer legal rights and reduced access to ameliorative resources. Although socio-economic disadvantage clearly affects boys as well as girls, gendered discrepancies ensure that girls have also to contend with the dice being frequently loaded against them.

In countries with high economic resources, Green and Taylor (2010) refer to a variety of studies which generally show that statistically boys and girls experience similar levels of psychological distress but for different reasons (e.g. Sweeting and West, 2002; Torsheim et al., 2006). As a result, and possibly predictably, boys are more likely to be diagnosed with conduct disorders and girls with emotional difficulties, including eating disorders.

It also needs to be noted that the entrenched and multi-layered discrimination faced by Indigenous boys and girls in 'rich' nations such as Australia and Canada has had a profound effect (NSW Aboriginal Mental Health Policy, 1997; CSDH, 2008). In the context of the mental health of Indigenous young people and children in Canada, Mussell et al. (2004) point to the need to recognize the serious impact of colonization and the negative consequences for Indigenous children when they are forced to attend residential schools. They highlight how these factors have served to disrupt family and community relationships, to suppress and de-value culture and traditional healing patterns, and to destroy individual and community self-respect and self-esteem. They emphasize the importance of enabling Indigenous communities to re-forge community identities, to foster links within and between communities, and to prioritize ecological and community-level responses to mental distress and ill-health. They also exhort policy makers and practitioners not to fall into the trap of 'blaming the victim' and pathologizing both individuals and communities for the problems experienced.

In Australia, persistent discrimination, the aftermath of policies which led to the 'stolen generation' (where between the 1920s and the 1960s Aboriginal children of 'mixed race' were forcibly removed from Aboriginal families and communities and placed with white families and in white institutions) and high levels of socio-economic disadvantage have resulted in similar issues being faced by Aboriginal communities. The effects are now being recognized in policy and emphasis has been placed, particularly by the Rudd and Gillard Labor Governments on addressing social exclusion (Commonwealth of Australia, 2009). State and Federal policy documents are also increasingly acknowledging Aboriginal views of mental health and are prioritizing community-orientated approaches and the rights of Aboriginal people (NSW Aboriginal

Mental Health Policy, 1997; A Stronger Fairer Australia, 2009). However, change is slow, and Aboriginal girls and boys overall have poorer educational opportunities and, particularly in rural areas, have to contend with limited access to infrastructure resources such as transport, the availability of healthy food and general health care. They also have to face the pervasive effects of ongoing generational devaluation as well as high mortality rates, with life expectancy being around 17 years lower than that for non-Indigenous Australians. In a survey carried out by Zubrick et al. (2005) into the social and emotional wellbeing of Aboriginal children and young people in the 4–17 age range in Western Australia, Aboriginal children were regarded as being nearly 10 per cent more likely than non-Aboriginal children to experience mental distress. In this survey, those factors identified as being more likely to protect the mental health of Aboriginal children included growing up in communities with a strong adherence to traditional culture and its way of life and living in households with a number of parental figures. The emphasis placed by Indigenous Australians on social and emotional well-being rather than mental health has also brought into question the applicability of westernized medicalized models. In contrast to clinical responses, the importance of inclusive strategies that take full account of the social, emotional and spiritual well-being of the whole community and the strong bond that exists with the land as well as the effects, both short and long term, of persistent discrimination and oppression is brought to the fore.

The construction of disorders: ADHD

As we have seen throughout this book, it is too simplistic to present medicalized and social approaches to mental distress as binary opposites or to conceptualize these as unitary and bounded entities. However, notwithstanding these provisos, it is important to recognize that diverse understandings position a child differently. As mentioned earlier in this chapter, it can be argued that an increasing number of individual behaviours are being both problematized and medicalized. In relation to young boys in particular, this point can be illustrated by focusing on Attention Deficit Hyperactivity Disorder, or ADHD; a diagnosis which has risen considerably over the last decade. It is notable that whereas in the 1970s and 1980s young boys who fidgeted and perhaps shouted out in class and who appeared relatively impervious to instruction would have been viewed as restless, as non-academic and as a 'handful', in the second decade of the twenty-first century, the same behaviours are increasingly being diagnosed as ADHD. These changes have provoked a series of responses. These range from emphasis being placed on newly discovered genetic and physiological behavioural determinants, to the view that compliance-orientated practices bring to the fore greater numbers of children who do not 'fit' particular class room regimes. Explanatory rationales also include more pronounced 'moral panics' about a relaxation in the control of children, particularly boys; changed responses to behaviour which is out of step with family circumstances; and effective drug company advertising campaigns.

ADHD is a 'condition' which always provokes discussion and which generates strong views from all quarters. Perhaps, one aspect to highlight is that human behaviour and interaction are complex and multi-faceted. Identifying an aspect as problematic, itself an activity which incorporates a range of views, value judgements and cultural and social processes, can result in a variety of solutions being put forward. Clearly subjecting behaviours regarded as problematic to a medicalized frame of reference with possible genetic or physiological causative factors have advantages. Behaviours regarded as difficult in a particular context are rendered containable and treatable, and it is the individual, rather than parents, family members, school environments and communities, who is regarded as requiring attention. A medicalized response can also favour early intervention as a way of identifying and treating a condition as early as possible in order to prevent further individual dysfunction and social problems occurring. In relation to the example of ADHD, the existence of an individual pathology and the need for expert intervention are promoted by researchers such as Barkley (1990, 2000) and Selikowitz (2004), and over the last decade, ADHD has additionally been associated with a number of anti-social and harmful behaviours including substance abuse, criminal activities, family conflict and suicide, with these in turn serving to increase pressure for early diagnosis and treatment (Collins et al., 2006; Wright, 2010).

However, as indicated, perspectives vary and there are those who, from within medicalized frames of reference, question the reliability of the diagnostic process and the effect of the diagnostic gaze (e.g. Timimi, 2002). In the case of the latter, this refers to the high probability of finding what you are looking for, especially, as highlighted above, that behavioural parameters are inevitably influenced by values, expectations and situationally specific factors. Other commentators such as Conrad (2007) and Graham (2010) question the applicability of any kind of classificatory certainty and point to a range of intervening, influencing and constructing factors (Wright, 2010).

Although ADHD has attracted more controversy than other conditions diagnosed in childhood, such as anxiety disorders, depression, autism and those located within the psychotic frame of reference, the ongoing debates do prompt us to 'think outside the box' and to question previously accepted 'certainties'. They also, from within a medicalized frame of reference, bring into question the levels of reliability, objectivity and validity claimed for psychiatric diagnoses, particularly those relating to children, although it is useful to note that diagnoses of ADHD are now being applied to adults and older people and are seen as having life-long implications (Barkley, 2000, Levy et al., 2006).

In the field of mental health, the notion of evidence-based practice, as we have seen in Chapter 3, is extremely influential. As discussed, the relationship between evidence and practice is not as straightforward as it is sometimes presented and there are many intervening considerations. It is also clear that in some situations evidence-based practice has been used as a means of an agency or service committing to one approach and rolling this out in a 'one-size-fits-all' manner to the detriment of those using services. However, research is important and research findings do have considerable influence. Nonetheless, all research findings, in order to be used constructively and appropriately, have to be subject to critical scrutiny. This incorporates the need to look at how findings can be interpreted, the appraisal of 'taken-for-granted' views and the ways in which professional or 'expert' knowledge is subject to change over time. An example which we can use here is that of a much cited, rigorously researched and influential survey carried out by Sawyer et al. (2001).

The study carried out by Sawyer et al. (2001) drew from a sample of 4509 children aged between 4 and 17 years and identified 14 per cent as having mental health problems associated with three conditions. These were ADHD, conduct disorder and depressive disorder. These figures were associated with a one-year prevalence rate, and they found that ADHD accounted for 11 per cent, with depressive disorder and conduct disorder comprising the remaining 3 per cent. They also found that in relation to the 14 per cent identified as having either ADHD or a depressive or conduct disorder, the majority were more likely to live in low-income families with single or step-parents, to have parents who had left school at an early age and to have parents who were unemployed. They also reported that many of those with mental health problems experienced difficulties in other areas of their lives and, as a result, were seen to be at increased risk of suicidal behaviour. They noted that only 25 per cent of those identified as having mental health problems had attended a professional service in the six months prior to the research survey. Sawyer et al. (2001) used these findings to emphasize that child and adolescent mental health difficulties constitute an important public health problem in Australia. They also pointed to the need to find an appropriate balance between funding provided for clinical interventions for individual children and families and funding for preventative supports directed towards 'at-risk' groups.

This study and these findings on the one hand can be seen to have provided important signposts that can and have been used to shape child and adolescent mental health services in Australia and elsewhere. However, on the other, critical analysis indicates that there are other ways of interpreting the findings. This is not to posit the view that one interpretation is right and another wrong, but to highlight that nothing is perhaps as straightforward as an initial reading would suggest.

In terms of different ways of viewing the survey, it is notable that the researchers used the Manual for Child Behaviour Checklist or CBCL developed by Achenbach in 1991 to identify the prevalence of the three disorders cited. This checklist, which is a screening rather than a diagnostic tool, was completed by parents, predominantly mothers, in relation to their children. The checklist findings were then linked to the parent version of the Diagnostic Interview Schedule for Children Version IV, which is based on the *Diagnostic and Statistical Manual of Mental Disorders IV*. In the light of these process details, rather than emphasis being placed on the production of verifiable statistical information, it is possible to direct attention towards the interpretative roles played by both the mothers and researchers and to the unquestioning acceptance of certain values and assumptions.

A critical analysis of the links made between low socioeconomic status, poor schooling, mixed models of parenting and a higher prevalence of the three disorders investigated indicates other possibilities to the one foregrounded. It can be suggested, for example, that mothers living in difficult circumstances and subject to high levels of stress, when asked, would be more likely to view the behaviour of their children as problematic. The targeted, individually orientated focus of the survey instruments would also orientate the mothers towards concentrating on the specific behaviour of their children rather than upon family matters generally or upon prevailing structural inequalities and social exclusionary factors such as low income, lack of employment opportunities, under-resourced schools and lack of quality pre-school child care.

In the Study, it is also notable that the researchers make a clear association between the three conditions investigated and the mental health of children and young people generally. They claim that 'if a wider range of disorders had been investigated, a higher prevalence of mental disorder would have been identified in the survey' (Sawyer et al., 2001). This is a significant claim and one which is based on extrapolation or an 'if' and 'would' scenario. Nevertheless, this claim and others like it do serve to influence the prevailing view that an increasing number of children are experiencing mental ill-health. As highlighted, whilst some researchers would accept these claims, others would query the connections and interrogate the implications. We argue that it is imperative in an evidence-based culture to critically appraise research findings and to consider different interpretations. This is not a recipe for inaction, but one which ensures that all research is used with appropriate provisos and qualifications.

This discussion effectively moves us on to an appraisal of 'risk' in relation to the mental health of children. 'Risk' is often described in policy documents and practice procedures in quantitative terms and is presented as being amenable to the application of rationale, objective and scientific criteria. Accordingly, the management of 'risk' is often ascribed a specific concrete quality with the influence of factors relating to uncertainty, varying values and assumptions being downgraded. 'Risk' also is predominantly viewed as negative rather than positive. In relation to children, growing up necessitates the taking of risks and what may be viewed as unacceptable or 'too risky' by one adult may be regarded by another and indeed by a child as an essential part of childhood. Similarly, the downplaying of children's ability to cope with 'risk' can also serve to heighten perceived risk factors.

Clinical frames of reference often fail to take account of what matters to children and frequently place them in a subordinate position. As a result, there is a continued tendency for mental health issues in relation to children to be individualized and to be addressed in a non-inclusive manner. This is despite, as highlighted elsewhere in this book, consumer-defined definitions of recovery gaining ground, community-oriented mental health survivor movements, prioritizing citizenship, gaining momentum (Beresford, 2000; Sayce, 2000; Beresford, 2006) and developments such as 'postpsychiatry', reconfiguring traditional notions of psychiatry and clinical practice (Perkins and Repper, 1999; Bracken and Thomas, 2005). The Mental Health Foundation (2007) recommends that rather than individual children being identified for attention and intervention, holistic approaches, which locate the whole child in their environment, and which provide a viable and productive form of constructive support, should be prioritized. As highlighted earlier, schools are seen to play a critical part in this process and whole-school approaches to mental health promotion, which include resourced anti-bullying strategies, have been found to be protective of children's mental health (Fraser and Blishen, 2007). Similarly, communities, be they geographical communities, communities of interest or other forms of communities, have a valuable role to play and can be strongly instrumental in fostering a sense of belonging and mutuality.

Current provision for children

Although there is a growing impetus for the mental health of children to be addressed more inclusively and holistically, policy and practice in this area continues to predominantly reflect traditional individualized diagnosis and treatment patterns and, with some minor changes, specialized tiered services.[1] This is in the context of mental health services for children in both the United Kingdom and Australia overall continuing to be reported as being beset by fragmentation and under-resourcing and as being hampered by age restrictions and eligibility criteria (Fawcett et al., 2004; Golightley, 2008).

To return to the topic of 'Early Intervention', this is clearly an area currently being prioritized in policy and practice in both United Kingdom and Australian contexts. McGorry and Young (2003) and Petersen et al. (2005), from within a clinical frame of reference, promote early intervention and regard it as an important means of reducing longer term distress. Birchwood (2000), in particular, points to the importance of sustaining early intervention for a minimum of three years following first diagnosis in order to prevent or limit the possibility of further decline. However, in relation to the current provision of early intervention services, there have been a number of difficulties reported. These relate to the accessibility of appropriate support systems and the unacceptability of some services to children and their parents in terms of service design and the clinical approach taken. It is also clear that many services have failed to engage and to consistently work with both children and their parents (Kurtz, 2003; McGorry et al., 2007). Additionally, Fawcett et al. (2004) draw attention to the possibility of early intervention serving to lock children into mental health careers with a concomitant singular interpretation of subsequent challenges. This can have significant implications for a child. It can serve to override personal and family responsiveness to behaviours and incidents. It can also result in a child's personality becoming absorbed into the diagnosed condition. On both counts, the erection of disabling barriers, which have the potential to limit aspirations, personal autonomy and choice, becomes a real possibility.

In terms of moving forward, although Fraser and Blishen (2007) comment specifically on the situation in the United Kingdom, their analysis and recommendations can be seen to

---

[1] It is recognized that, in England especially, the continued implementation of the National Services Framework Standards (2004) is placing emphasis on the broadening out of tier one which refers to the provision of general advice and treatment.

have a clear resonance in Australia. They point to Children's Trusts (or Community Services in Australia) and Child and Adolescent Mental Health Services (CAMHS) not always working together as effectively as they could. They also draw attention to the key role played by the voluntary sector and to how, in the UK context, non-government organizations have shown themselves to be in a position to deliver the services that children and young people say they want and find helpful and to operate more responsively. They therefore point to the importance of voluntary sector organizations working with children's services, as well as with educational and health departments, to ensure that their often unique and innovative contribution influences mainstream responses. They acknowledge that this form of collaborative working requires renewed attention to be paid to a number of areas. These include the breaking down of boundaries, the formulation of new partnerships, the paying of attention to different and innovative approaches, as well as all professionals in the field of children's services actively expressing a commitment to working together.

Concluding remarks

Ensuring the positive mental health of children has a global resonance. We maintain that attention has to be paid to the ever-increasing pressures which children are subject to and we support inclusive practices. However, we argue that 'problem' identification is influenced by a variety of aspects associated with context, gender, class and culture and that responses also vary depending on the professional perspective adopted and the resources which can be accessed. As a result, we emphasize that the varying ways in which children can be positioned and behaviours interpreted have to be subject to ongoing critical review. In Chapter 5, we continue to explore these themes by focusing more specifically on adolescents and their views of what works for them. We also advocate for a greater range of holistic support services that concentrate on strengths and which engage children, young people, parents, schools and communities in constructive action.

CHAPTER 5

Trying Times for Adolescents: Fight, Flight or Compliance?

As we have seen in Chapter 4, recent research in both the United Kingdom and Australia has provided a range of statistics which show that increasing numbers of young people are experiencing mental distress (Meltzer et al., 2000; Green et al., 2005; The Mental Health Foundation, 2007; Commonwealth of Australia, 2009). The World Health Organization has estimated that globally one in eight young people is given a mental health diagnosis and one in 20 is regarded as experiencing behavioural, developmental or emotional difficulties (WHO, 2005).

To give more detail, Rowling (2006) points out that in Australia it has been estimated that two in every five young people in the community suffers from a depressed mood in any six-month period and that young people are at greatest risk of experiencing mental health problems. In Australia, annual statistics show around 20 per cent of young people being classified as having a disorder associated with anxiety, substance abuse or depression (ABS, 2007), and the Australian Government (2010) states that one in four young Australians will experience mental illness in any one year. In the United Kingdom, The Mental Health Foundation has noted a 70 per cent increase in diagnosed rates of anxiety and depression over the last 25 years, with up to 1 in 15 young people reporting self-harming behaviours. Within Australia, additional pressures can be seen to be brought to bear on young people living in rural areas, with 16 per cent of rural young people (16–19 years) compared to 13 per cent in capital cities not fully participating in education or work (ABS, 2005) and, as we have seen in Chapter 4, Indigenous young people are subject to a range of adverse statistics. In this chapter, we continue to explore the areas raised in Chapter 4, but focus specifically on those aspects which particularly relate to adolescents.

Who is an adolescent?

Although adolescence or the term 'young person' is usually regarded as referring to the teenage years between 13 and 19, administrative definitions vary. For example, as McGorry et al. (2007) point out, the Australian Bureau of Statistics defines a 'young person' as an individual aged between 12 and 25 years. The Australian Institute of Health and Welfare focuses on the period from 12 to 24 whilst the United Nations regards 'young people' as those aged between 15 and 24 years. In the United Kingdom, young people tend to be defined as those between the ages of 16 and 24 (The Mental Health Foundation, 2007). In this chapter, although the variation in age ranges used in surveys and in studies has to be acknowledged, particular attention will be paid to young people in the 16–24-year age group.

Pressures placed on adolescents

The growth in the number of young people experiencing mental distress, as we have seen in Chapter 3, can be attributed to a range of factors. These include greater attention being paid in schools to issues relating to mental health and mental ill-health with the result that more young people seek help; the rise in the range of pressures placed on adolescents generally; and, as also discussed in Chapter 3, an increasingly medicalized response to emotional and social problems.

With regard to the particular pressures placed on adolescents, as previously discussed with regard to children, peer pressure, media images, high expectations, together with the insecurity of the job market and the spiralling cost of higher education (Alston and Kent, 2006) can increase the risk of young people experiencing mental distress and social exclusion (Jeffrey and McDonnell, 2004; Shucksmith, 2004).

The Mission Australia (2009a, 2011) snapshots, also referred to in Chapter 3, show that young people rank body image, drugs and family conflict as key concerns and these are reported as affecting a quarter of all respondents. Sexuality is also mentioned, with discrimination and prejudice faced by those attracted to the same sex featuring significantly and adding to the levels of mental distress experienced. In terms of mental health issues generally, one respondent comments: 'I'm mostly concerned with the challenges youth face – being themselves, being accepted for who they are, stress and mental health.' Another said: 'Being a Gen Y, I believe I have achieved a lot for my age. I have learnt to work hard, reap the benefits, but not how to deal with stress' (Mission Australia, Snapshot, 2009a: 2, 3).

It is also pertinent to note that although women appear in mental health statistics more frequently than men (Prior, 1999), with regard to young people, boys are increasingly being recorded as experiencing difficulties as frequently and sometimes more frequently, than girls (Social Trends 2010; Social Exclusion Unit, 2005), and that in Australia, young rural men in towns with populations of less than 4000 are twice as likely than urban youth to take their own lives (Bourke, 2001; AIHW, 2010). The reasons for this are unclear, although it may relate to boys generally being less inhibited than girls in terms of exhibiting their feelings through their behaviour and as a consequence attracting more attention. Conversely, it could relate to boys having greater difficulty in expressing their emotions than girls, resulting in greater stress and tension being experienced.

It is also notable that the Mission Australia (2009a, 2011) snapshots highlight issues relating to suicide and self-harm. Although numbers are small overall, suicide is the second highest cause of death amongst young people in Australia with, as highlighted above, more young men than young women committing suicide (AIHW, 2010). However, the number of young people who self-harm is both far higher and is increasing, with the rate for young women generally being twice as high as that for young men. Figures show that during the 2005–2006 period in Australia, over 7000 young people in the 12–24-year-old age group were hospitalized as a result of intentional self-harm (AIHW, 2008; Mission Australia, 2009a, Snapshot). One respondent in the Mission Australia (2009a) Snapshot survey remarked: 'I have a great deal of concern surrounding the issues of self harm and suicide.

Dealing with self harming issues myself I have found services limited and public systems with lack of understanding and compassion shattering any remaining self worth of the individuals who seek such help' (Mission Australia, 2009a, Snapshot: 3).

The voices of young people captured in these snapshot surveys emphasize that adolescence is a period of rapid transition. It is a period when young people are experimenting with behaviours, image and identities, when established relationships require renegotiation and when pressures from peers, schools and parents can be profound. Adolescence is also a period which can be linked to experimental behaviours such as unsafe sex, alcohol and substance abuse and anti-social and criminal activities.

The issues involved are such that many commentators refer to adolescence as a period of risk. Coleman and Hagell (2007) point out, for example, that risk takes many forms and can be exacerbated by factors such as poverty, deprivation, illness or problematic family backgrounds, with the latter including young people who have experienced abuse or neglect and those who have been placed in the care system. Indeed, the Mission Australia (2009b) Snapshot, focusing on how living arrangements impact on the experiences of young people, noted that those in 'out of home care' highlight physical and sexual abuse, coping with stress and depression, problematic perceptions of body image and the possibility of suicide as major areas requiring action.

When looking at the issues facing young people, an important aspect to consider relates to how the changes associated with adolescence are viewed both by young women and men as well as by significant others. Shyness, for example, can be experienced as a severe social impediment, as an inconvenient but transitory phase or as something that a young person manages on a daily basis. It can be viewed as an anxiety disorder, as part of growing up or as related to levels of resilience. Its severity can in turn be linked to personal perception as well as to perceived incapacity. Different family members and professionals may also have different responses, ranging from shyness being seen as a sign of intellectual ability, as a protective way of responding to peer group pressure, as something which is trivial and not worth taking account of, or as a condition which requires professional support and intervention. Vostanis (2007) warns against focusing on a narrow behaviour in isolation from how a young person is generally developing and functioning. He emphasizes the importance of looking at the impact of a behaviour, trait or emotion regarded by the young person or by others as problematic in the context of a young person's life overall. This comment is given further impetus by the work of psychiatrists Bracken and Thomas (2005), whose work is referred to in Chapters 1 and 2. They maintain that psychiatry's emphasis on 'methodological individualism' is based on the assumption that particular diagnoses represent the correct way to view forms of mental distress. These in turn are regarded as having a universal applicability regardless of context. Bracken and Thomas (2005) maintain that these perspectives and practices serve to diminish and erode individuals, their individuality and the contexts in which they live their lives. They counter the view that different psychological states can be examined in isolation from the world around them and maintain that contextual issues relating to embodiment (i.e. the ongoing relationship between mind and body), enculturement (which refers to the linguistic, cultural and political reality of society) and temporal matters (which relates to lives being viewed as always being in flux, never fixed and always involved in a journey from past to future) are of prime importance.

Resilience

Over recent years, the concept of resilience has gained momentum and is increasingly being applied to a wider range of areas. Examples include the work of Martin and Marsh (2006) who focus on educational settings and Rayner and Montague (2000) who examine resilience in relation to child care. With regard to mental health, the exploration of resilience is serving to re-emphasize a more holistic understanding of well-being (Coleman and Hagell, 2007).

Resilience in young people is generally regarded as being promoted by internal and external factors. Protective factors are associated with coping strategies which include self-efficacy, the ability to engage in self-reflection, a self-reliant attitude, being able to maintain a positive outlook and a well-developed ability to address and solve problems. Positive experiences of enduring relationships, a secure and nurturing family environment, good levels of social and educational attainment, being able to generate positive responses from others and the ability to make friends are also regarded as key attributes. Many of these aspects are clearly interrelated and educational attainment, for example, is likely to increase self-esteem, leading to a range of positive experiences. Those aspects which can have a negative effect include the reverse side of those areas referred to above, so parental incapacity and its implications, together with a lack of emotional support from significant others and peers, can reduce self-esteem, confidence and lead to a range of negative experiences (Mills and Frost, 2007; Vostanis, 2007). Olsson et al. (2003) make a distinction between resilience as an outcome and resilience as a process. They note that where research is predominantly concerned with outcomes, emphasis is placed on factors such as self-esteem, social competence and good mental health and on how these factors can enable young people to respond positively to risk and to difficult situations. When resilience is viewed as a process, the focus shifts to those aspects which ameliorate the impact of risk or adversity. Coleman and Hagell (2007) draw attention to the importance of process as a means of both resourcing and facilitating forms of support which serve to enhance and strengthen protective forces.

Resilience is a concept which is often explored at the level of the individual rather than at social levels. A consequence of placing emphasis on the individual to the exclusion of wider social forces is that the ways in which social positioning and social disadvantage affect young people can become obscured. The WHO 'Mental Health, Resilience and Inequalities' Report (2009) adopts a social perspective and looks at mental health and resilience in the context of communities. This Report emphasizes that poor mental health is both a cause and a consequence of social, economic and environmental inequalities. It highlights that the adverse impact of stress is greater in societies where significant inequalities exist and where some people feel worse off than others. The Report emphasizes that levels of mental distress among communities need to be understood as a response to inequalities involving relative deprivation across society rather than solely in terms of individual pathology. It recommends establishing viable partnerships between health and other sectors to address social and economic problems that act as a catalyst for mental distress. This incorporates identifying and reducing barriers to social contact by developing policy and practice responses to adversity that address contributory factors such as poverty, unemployment and environmental constraints. It also involves actively promoting mental well-being by putting the social back into public spaces and supporting local initiatives such as community transport schemes, neighbourhood gardens and local festivals and ensuring that young people are fully included in decision-making processes at all levels.

In a similar manner, the World Health Organization's 2009 Report entitled 'Mental health, resilience and inequalities' (Friedli, 2009) focuses on the social determinants of good mental health. This Report emphasizes that mental health is a fundamental element of resilience, health assets, capabilities and positive adaptation and that emotional well-being plays a central role in relation to young people's life chances. Protective assets are seen to include self-esteem, self-efficacy, readiness to learn and a positive social identity and these are regarded as influencing a wide range of health and social outcomes. Mental health is also viewed as a key pathway through which inequality impacts on health and the Report points to overwhelming evidence of inequality being not only a cause of stress in itself but as also exacerbating the difficulties involved in coping with material deprivation. The statement 'Mental health is produced socially: the presence or absence of mental health is above all a social indicator and therefore requires social, as well as individual solutions' makes it clear that mental health is a social and community responsibility and that resilience is socially generated (Freidli, 2009: 38).

It is clearly important to locate resilience within the parameters of structural and social disadvantage. However, if relatively straightforward predictive measures are used as a means of fostering social inclusion and addressing social exclusion, then there can be pitfalls. MacDonald (2007) explores resilience in the context of risk and social inclusion and criticizes the ways in which social inclusion policies have attempted to address disadvantage by employing predictive measures and actively seeking to identify those young people at greatest risk of remaining socially excluded throughout their adult lives. He notes how research, such as that produced by Brynner and Parsons (2002), has been used to make direct links between cause and effect. As a result, not being in training or education at age 16, for example, has been widely used in policy and practice documents as a means of predicting a range of exclusionary experiences. These include adult unemployment, experiencing trouble with the law, teenage pregnancy and poorer mental health. In a similar way, drawing from research carried out by Farrington (1994), MacDonald (2007) highlights how the identification of behavioural problems in some children has been promoted as a means of identifying and controlling 'risk' behaviour for all young people. He maintains that whilst concepts of risk and resilience are valuable in understanding the diverse experiences and outcomes for young people generally, the application of predictive measures to individual young women and men is far less straightforward. This, he asserts, results from relatively little attention being paid to changing historical and social contexts, to an over reliance on individual pathology and to insufficient attention being given to changing local allegiances. In a similar fashion, he pertinently states that not all young people who score highly on social exclusion indices will feel socially excluded, nor will they necessarily enter adulthood with social exclusional careers.

Early intervention

A discussion of the possible pitfalls of predictive factors leads us into a further exploration of early intervention and the ways in which this strategy is increasingly being promoted within policy and practice documents and procedures as a means of reducing the intensity, duration and impact of mental health difficulties. As highlighted in Chapter 4, particular weight is currently being given to early intervention strategies as a means of effectively managing the mental ill-health of young people. It is clear that a number of research projects indicate that early detection and intervention for young people experiencing instability in their mental health correlates with more favourable outcomes in both the short and the long term (e.g. The Mental Health Foundation, 1999; Birchwood, 2000; Johnson et al., 2000; Davis et al., 2006). The Australian Government in its 2010 social inclusion document entitled 'A Stronger, Fairer Australia', as well as supporting mental health promotion and mental ill-health prevention programmes, is also rolling out a number of early intervention measures through its 'Mind Matters and Kids Matters' initiatives. However, it is notable that a range of researchers including Bentall and Morrison (2002), Warner (2008), Spandler and Carlton (2009) question the efficacy of early intervention and the almost automatic association between early intervention and positive outcomes. They also draw attention to the tensions which exist between early intervention policies and practices and the very different strategies employed by those engaged in mental health promotion and prevention. These researchers draw from their research findings to maintain that the evidence as to the effectiveness of early intervention is at best weak and at worst non-existent. Spandler and Carlton (2009) state, 'such practices raise a number of "human rights" issues regarding the potential of exposing people to a psychiatric career' and 'the inherent uncertainties regarding prognosis in the administration of drugs with potentially harmful side-effects to people who may not go on to develop psychosis' (Spandler and Carlton, 2009: 247).

It is also notable that despite the emphasis currently being placed on early intervention, far less attention is being paid to the nature of the intervention provided, to the resulting outcomes and to how forms of early intervention are viewed by recipients. Drawing from the critical insights provided by MacDonald (2007) given above, it is also important to acknowledge that early intervention programmes tend to be underpinned by a strong belief in the efficacy and objectivity of clinical diagnostic procedures and the existence of a direct relationship between cause and effect. This is not to assert that the clinical identification of a mental health condition and an early response will not mitigate the later severity or the possible consequences in terms of a poor unemployment record and relationship difficulties, but to draw attention to other intervening factors which, for some young women and men, might render early intervention, diagnosis and treatment problematic.

Current service provision and the voices of young people

Fraser and Blishen (2007) in the United Kingdom and Boyd et al. (2006) and Patel et al. (2007) in Australia have highlighted that for young people living in urban and rural areas, the period of transition from childhood into adulthood is the time when they need most support. However, it is also a period when services, due to a lack of availability, accessibility or 'fit' from a young person's perspective, are least able to respond. A Report produced by the Social Exclusion Unit in the United Kingdom in 2005 acknowledged that the ways in which young people become adults has become more complicated and diverse and that policies and services have generally failed to keep up with such changes. Inconsistent age barriers and a lack of integration between different service sectors, under-funding and little information on service outcomes have been highlighted as ongoing problem areas. This has left many young people having to either try to access adult services or to experience an unsupported transition between services specifically provided for children and young people and those available to adults. Similarly, the four-tier Children and Adolescent Mental Health Services (CAMHS) model used in the United Kingdom and also to some extent in Australia, which moves from generalized mental health services to highly specialized input, has been seen both as overloaded and as not sufficiently responding to what young people say they need (Fraser and Blishen, 2007). In the United Kingdom, as well as in Australia, CAMHS were not established to provide a comprehensive service nor to cater for all the mental health needs of young people, yet these services are not only often left to take sole responsibility for all the mental health needs of young people but are also criticized for failing to do an impossible job. Similarly, although as in the United Kingdom the promotion of positive mental health is seen to be a key priority and more money has been forthcoming, resources in both Australia and the United Kingdom overall remain stretched and inadequate.

Associated with the pressures placed on CAMHS, research carried out by Howarth and Street (2000), Young Minds (2000) and Kurtz (2003) has further indicated that mental health professionals consistently experience difficulties in working with young people diagnosed as experiencing moderate to severe mental health problems because a significant number refuse to engage in therapeutic or support programmes. This has relevance to the situation in Australia, alluded to by Rowling and Taylor (2005), and highlights the tendency for young people to confide in peers, not adults, if there is a fear of losing control over what happens to them. These studies and reports have also emphasized that young people believe that they are not listened to or supported, that they feel intimidated by psychiatrists and that requirements to meet tightly defined criteria exclude many of them from seeking help and accessing support. In these studies, young people have also drawn attention to the need to build trust, to maintain confidentiality and for professionals and support workers to have personal experience of mental distress so that they can actively engage with a young person and focus on their definition of the problem (Fraser and Blishen, 2007).

The position of young people in the 16–24 age range can be seen to be pivotal to these current debates. The studies which look at what young people experiencing mental distress say they want and would find useful refer to both social and holistic factors, as well as to a range of specific measures for promoting mental health and responding to mental distress (e.g. The Mental Health Foundation, 1997, 2001, 2005, 2007 (UK); The Youth Affairs Council of South Australia, 2006).

Vostanis (2007) notes that 'mental health' is often regarded as an adult term with little meaning for young people. He comments:

Considering the lack of clarity among services and professionals on what constitutes mental health and the remit of each service in relation to adolescent mental health (from promotion to specialist services), it comes as little surprise that this confusion filters down to the young people themselves.

(Vostanis, 2007: 92)

Reports (which include the 'Young Minds Stressed Out and Struggling Project Report', 2004; The Mental Health Foundation Reports produced in 2001, 2004 and 2007; the Young Minds Report, 2006; the Youth Affairs Council of South Australia Report, 2006; the findings of James, 2007; and the Mission Australia Snapshots, 2009a, 2009b and 2011) reinforce the imperative of promoting good mental health rather than just preventing ill-health and of the development of a range of flexible, holistic, easily accessible forms of support which serve the needs of all young people and which involve schools, communities and families in a variety of ways, using a variety of mediums and resources.

The importance of providing information and support so that family and friends know what to do when a young person experiences mental distress has been particularly highlighted by the Mission Australia Snapshot (2008), by ORYGEN Youth Health, Australia, and by Headspace, the National Youth Mental Health Foundation of Australia (2009). These Reports and Surveys have not only reviewed wide-ranging mental health promotion measures for all young people, but have also drawn attention to the shape young people experiencing mental distress or who have been diagnosed with a mental health condition want mental health support services to take. As highlighted above, particular emphasis is placed on the provision of person centred, inclusive support services which are flexible enough to provide easily accessible provision with a 24-hour remit, which use the Internet and which can adapt to the frequently volatile circumstances of young people's lives. Young women and men have also drawn attention to the utility of buddy schemes with accompanying support systems and to easy access to a number of options at a range of levels. The Reports also suggest that if young people are fully involved in the development of services, they are likely to put forward ideas which are creative and innovative and which focus on moving away from traditional service structures (Mental Health Foundation, 2001, 2004, 2007; Young Minds, 2006). The Mental Health Foundation, 'Listen Up! Report' (2007) stresses that young people want less emphasis to be placed on mainstream health and social care interventions and greater attention to be paid to those focusing, for example, on arts, creativity, leisure, participation, sport, education and spirituality. This Report highlights that young people experiencing mental distress said that the voluntary sector was the place they looked to for responsive, non-bureaucratic and welcoming services and that they wanted existing services to change to better meet their needs. Young people also want to be actively involved in service design and delivery with this including participation in the selection of staff, in deciding how budgets are spent and in determining how services are organized. All of these Reports strongly state that unless services are designed and operate in such a way that young people actually want to engage with them, they will not be successful (Table 5.1).

All of these Reports recommend that although specialist services are required for complex or serious mental health issues, these need to be specifically tailored to young people and to take full account of their views about what works for them. Similarly, the Reports emphasize that the basic service model for young people needs fundamental change with attention being paid to inclusivity, to strengths-based approaches and to moving away from negative categorization processes. This draws attention to the importance of services being designed *with* young people, with emphasis being placed on the forms of support which young

Table 5.1 What services do young people say they want?

The sorts of services young people say they want include:

- Places to go that are informal, are open in the evenings, work on a drop-in rather than an appointment basis and are staffed by skilled youth workers with a detailed or personal knowledge of mental health issues.
- Services targeted at 16–25-year-olds to be 'young-people-friendly' in design and approach and to use the Internet.
- Telephone helplines to be available at night, in the evenings and at weekends, staffed by skilled telephone counsellors who know what the local support options are for young people.
- Access to reflexology and acupuncture which are available to many adults experiencing mental distress but are difficult to access for young people.
- A choice of workers so that a young person can build a rapport with someone who understands their individual situation.
- Peer support in schools and youth work settings which have easy access to 'young people' friendly counselling services in schools.

Source: Fraser and Blishen (2007)

people feel they can use, rather than the requirements of existing structures and services taking priority.

Concluding remarks

Adolescence is a time when young people are experiencing profound changes and periods of transition and are subject to powerful emotions. It is a time when they are obliged to re-negotiate their position within families, with peers, in educational settings and to prove their worth in a variety of academic, sporting and vocational capacities. Across the globe, mental distress amongst young people is seen to be increasing significantly and although the reasons for this are not straightforward, it is of considerable concern that mental health services for young people continue to be described as fragmented, under-resourced and inadequately staffed and as lacking the capacity to respond to young people experiencing mental distress in the ways that they want. Young people comprise a service user/consumer group at a critical life stage who are frequently not involved in discussions about their understandings, experiences or views of services and who have not, to date, had a distinctive voice in the debates surrounding mental health. A member of the ORYGEN Youth Health Platform Team in Australia maintains:

> Our health system needs to take the next step forward in removing the barriers between health professionals and young people. It needs to start listening to what we are saying and what we are asking for. To know what works best for us, the system has to become youth-friendly and youth-orientated

(James, 2007: 58)

This provides not only a challenge, but also requires a significant shift in thinking. Clearly, the future of mental health services for young people requires further negotiation. In Chapter 6, we look at how many of the themes raised in this chapter relate to adults and consider innovative developments in the field.

Adults: The Terrain of Mental Ill-Health

As we have seen with children and young people, recent statistics in the Western world show an apparent rise in the number of adults experiencing mental ill-health. For example, the NHS Confederation (2009) indicates that the proportion of the adult English population diagnosed with a mental disorder has increased from 15.5 per cent in 1993 to 17.6 per cent in 2007. The Mental Health Foundation (2009) equates this to 1 in 6 people in England suffering from a common mental health problem, and their report also draws attention to depression and anxiety rising by a fifth amongst middle-aged women. Similarly, the Australian Bureau of Statistics (ABS) (2009) indicates that in 2007 45 per cent of Australians aged between 16 and 85 years had at some point in their lives experienced mental ill-health and that 1 in 5 Australians have been diagnosed with a mental disorder. The types of mental disorder alluded to in these surveys range from psychotic diagnoses such as schizophrenia and bipolar disorders, to depression and anxiety, to substance use disorders. Whilst more women than men are reported as experiencing anxiety disorders, more men than women meet the criteria for substance use disorders. Over the last few decades, general trends have shown the predominance of women over men in mental health statistics. However, recent figures produced by the ABS (2009) are pointing to a changing trend with more men than women being diagnosed with a mental disorder during their lifetime and to this often being alcohol related.

The experiences of those diagnosed as experiencing a mental disorder will vary considerably, but the ABS Report (2009) draws attention to a general negative impact on family life, work ability and social interaction. These aspects can often lead to social isolation and the statistics show that people with a diagnosed mental disorder are more likely to live by themselves as a result of relationship difficulties. They also tend to be divorced, to have infrequent contact with family and friends and to experience higher levels of unemployment (ABS Report, 2009). However, it has been recorded that only a quarter of people in England experiencing mental distress seek professional help (The Mental Health Foundation, 2009). Similarly, in Australia nearly two-thirds of people with a diagnosed mental disorder fail to regularly access mental health services (ABS Report, 2009). The figures also show that people aged between 16 and 34 years are less likely to use mental health services (29%) than people in the 35–54 age group (41%) or those aged 55–85 years (37%). Women are also more likely than men to use mental health services (41% compared to 28% respectively), and people diagnosed with up to two disorders (53%) are more likely to use services than people diagnosed with just one disorder (24%).

Over the years, research and anecdotal evidence has highlighted differences between men and women in terms of both diagnosis and representation in the mental health system. Although, as indicated above, the situation appears to be changing, women have traditionally been more highly represented in the mental health statistics than men. Payne (1999) suggests that this may relate to particular pressures in their lives making them more susceptible to mental ill-health. For instance, lack of well-paid, non-casual employment, poverty, childbirth and pressures in later life, generally affect women more than men. In addition, Payne argues that women have been more likely to appear in the statistics because of discriminatory attitudes and practices within the mental health system. There is evidence to suggest that, in the past, health care practitioners may well have held stereotypical views of women and a narrow perspective of women's mental health status (Broverman et al., 1970).

In order to tease out the obvious and more subtle differences, it is important to consider the literature and research generated in the latter part of the twentieth century. In particular, this material can serve to illuminate gender issues and particular life stages set against the wider canvass of social and cultural inequalities.

A historical overview of women and mental health

In 1985, Novara, by means of a series of interviews with women service users and women health professionals, attempted to uncover whether the health system treated women differently from men. She commented, 'I found *three* definitive answers: yes, no, and maybe' (1985: 57). In contemporary times, as then, there is great diversity on this topic. Since 1985, new perspectives and parlance have been introduced and contemporary theory and practice incorporates anti-discriminatory and anti-oppressive perspectives. Such terms have seen currency in legislation and policy and current practice works towards minimizing the marginalization and bias that many believe has been working to disadvantage women in the past. This disadvantage has been seen through the prism of diagnosis and treatment (Chesler, 1972; Busfield, 1996) as well as by means of service needs and delivery (Rhodes et al., 2002; Scheyett and McCarthy, 2006).

In the two decades from the 1970s to the 1990s, feminists were actively engaged with issues relating to women and their relationship to psychiatry and a burgeoning literature emerged about gender, bias and historical disadvantage experienced by women in the mental health system (Chesler, 1972; Millett, 1974; Hare-Mustin, 1983; Showalter, 1985; Kaplan, 1988; Russell, 1995; Busfield, 1996; Jimenez, 1997). Russell (1995) argues that historically, women more than men have experienced biological psychiatry. In the nineteenth century, many of the identified forms of madness essentially could be called 'women's complaints'. In previous times, such complaints would be dealt with by female healers, but with the coupling of madness with medicine, male doctors began to categorize and treat such complaints (Russell, 1995).

In the nineteenth century, hysteria was the paradigmatic female mental condition and was widely diagnosed (Busfield, 1996). The latter part of that century has been called the 'golden age' of hysteria and as Goldstein (1987) notes was a period when the condition apparently flourished throughout Europe and the United States, crossing class barriers, and what was once an upper-class complaint became common amongst working-class women. With the roots of the term in the Greek word 'hysteron', meaning the womb, the inevitable gender connotation of the condition was clear. Hysteria was caused by a movement of the womb, but even when these ideas were rejected, hysteria continued to be diagnosed as a female condition (Veith, 1965). Towards the end of the nineteenth century, an increasing number of practitioners claimed that women were not the only hysterics and that there was male hysteria. Following Charcot, Freud rejected the view that hysteria was an exclusively female condition, but continuing support remained for this state to be associated with women and the terms 'hysterical' and 'feminine' were often used interchangeably (Showalter, 1987).

Showalter (1987) points out that in England by the end of the nineteenth century 'women had decisively taken the lead as psychiatric patients'. This trend also developed in Europe (Ripa, 1990) and in the United States (Ehrenreich and English, 1973). Some feminists have argued that assumptions about gender shape medical science, and in turn medical science reinforces gender (Fausto-Sterling, 1985; Theriot, 1993). Biological fundamentalism informed British psychiatry in this period (Showalter, 1987) and similar ideology informed American psychiatric thought about women's mental distress and mental illness. In her review of psychiatric conceptions of women and mental disorders in the years spanning 1960–1994, Jimenez (1997) found that a psychological model largely replaced the biological model that dominated earlier psychiatric thought. She argues that during this period of the mid-to-late twentieth century, new psychiatric categories were introduced and these privileged dominant values controlling gender-role behaviour in women.

According to Russell (1995), 'fashions' exist in terms of the conceptualization of women and mental distress. It is no longer acceptable to diagnose a woman with hysteria, but for some time in the late twentieth century, Premenstrual Syndrome (PMS) was in vogue to explain both biological and psychological distress in women (Tucker, 1991). Brown (1990) has suggested that psychiatry cannot explain why some diagnostic categories appear and disappear – and sometimes reappear in a different guise – and she highlights psychiatry's ongoing susceptibility to social and political factors and fashions.

In her research into psychiatric conceptualizations of mental disorders in women between 1960 and 1994, Jimenez (1997) found that new categories of mental disorder had been created to reflect the changing norms of gendered behaviour. Borderline and dependent personality disorders had become popular and in effect offered a psychological-moral ideology to limit behaviour for women, just as hysteria offered women normative guideposts in earlier years. The rise of PMS and Premenstrual Dysphoric Disorder (PMDD) continued to offer diagnoses rooted in the biological model of mental disorders. Jimenez (1997) claims that gender-based psychiatric conceptions, relying on psychological and reproductive ideas, have the potential to control women. In her words, 'Psychiatry's ideas about appropriate gender-role behavior are hardly unique. What is unique is its role in the social construction of disease: Through the reification of its diagnostic system, psychiatry translates gender ideologies into definable codes for women's behavior' (1997: 171).

Past and more recent research has pointed to differences between men and women in terms of service need and delivery (Hoppe, 1985; Novara, 1985; Russell, 1995; Arvidsson, 2009; Van Den Tillaart et al., 2009). Studies have shown that women's experiences of mental distress, their marginalization and having their stories discounted or not taken seriously have consequences which include silencing and rendering invisible women's physical health concerns (Mohr, 1999; Barnes et al., 2006). It is also notable that despite earlier recommendations from WHO (1978) regarding the need for health care to be provided to citizens in an equitable and comprehensive manner, evidence continues to show that health care provision remains a concern, particularly for marginalized people (Raphael, 2004; Morrow, 2006; WHO, 2009b). Meleis and Inn (2002) forward the idea that the mark of marginalization is 'the extent to which they (people) are stereotyped, rendered voiceless, silenced, not taken seriously, peripheralized, homogenized, ignored, dehumanized and ordered around' (Meleis and Inn, 2002: 96). Vasas (2005) notes that marginalization perhaps should be seen as a concept rather than a process. This manifests itself when 'helping professionals' treat women with mental health challenges as the 'other', thus leaving them on the fringes of health care. In this way, marginality can be perpetuated, often leaving women isolated from forms of support which they would find helpful.

A historical reflection which might be considered a truism when it comes to women and mental health relates to hearing their concerns. According to Currie, 'to truly understand how to deliver service one must first *listen* to the stories of those whose lives are affected' (quoted in Van Den Tillart et al., 2009: 161). Accordingly, it can be argued that only by listening closely to women's stories can needs and issues be revealed, with women's stories operating to reveal oppositions to constraining and powerful ideologies about women and the nature of their mental distress and ill-health.

Women's voices draw attention to the wide range of stressors which many are subject to. Many adult women who have lost a parent in childhood report depression in later life (McLeod, 1991). Similarly, multiple family disadvantages can have an effect and, as highlighted in the Newcastle '1000 families' study, can result in a greater likelihood of a diagnosis of depression in adulthood (Sadowski et al., 1999). In terms of a history of sexual abuse in childhood, women generally are more likely than men to make such reports, and many adult women who are later diagnosed with a mental health condition point to one or more episodes of sexual assault in childhood (Beitchman et al., 1991). In addition, the consequences and possible disadvantages for children whose mother has been diagnosed with depression and the effects of this on the quality of parenting have been the subject of a number of research projects (Murray, 1992; Pound, 1996; Hauck et al., 2008).

Becoming a parent is one stage in the life-cycle that can test coping skills and exacerbate stress. Generally speaking, for women, motherhood is a demanding as well as a life-changing experience. For those women who have been diagnosed with a mental health condition, the challenge of motherhood is amplified and they also risk the possible removal of their child (Oates, 1996; Lagan et al., 2009).

Social support can buffer against mental distress and provide much needed assistance to families (Fleming et al., 1992; Mares et al., 2005). Mothers who experience crises are also more likely to lose custody of their children if they have poor and inadequate family and community support networks (Ackerson, 2003; Howard et al., 2003; Reupert and Maybery, 2007). Conversely, mothers with a mental health diagnosis can experience additional pressures and stress when their social supports are intrusive and/or controlling of them (Nicholson et al., 1998). For practitioners working with mothers, the balancing act involves assistance and advocacy, reinforcing positive support networks and reducing adverse pressures. In her research into gender, ethnicity and mental health from the perspective of social workers, Barn argues that in the case of Bangladeshi women living in Britain '... needs and problems are conceptualized and contextualized within a holistic framework but are constrained by statutory frameworks' (2008: 79). She found that these constraints militated against fully meeting the needs of women and ensuring their welfare. She also reports that reconciling the demands and concerns of the organization with those of women service users proved to be a challenging task.

Exploring men and mental health status

Men, too, historically have faced challenges with regard to their mental health and mental ill-health. In 2001, Prior and Hayes (2001) noted that for the first time in the twentieth century in Britain, men outnumbered women in residential mental health facilities. For men and women alike, any exploration of mental ill-health needs to consider the broader social context and the uniquely gendered social expectations of the various life-stages.

Analysts such as Busfield (1996) and Prior (1999) have pointed out that the apparent disparities between men and women are not specifically related to gender but to power imbalances which women like men experience in diverse ways. Over time power imbalances have shifted and changed for many Western women, but this point makes a useful link to a discussion of men and mental health where, at the outset it needs to be emphasized that just as not all women experience the negative effects of power imbalances, not all men experience the reverse.

It is clear that gendered binaries, such as those relating to rationality and irrationality or reason and unreason, have clearly played a part in terms of what is seen to constitute acceptable and unacceptable behaviour and what, in relation to the expectations and limitations of prevailing social conventions, is regarded as requiring social control. As Busfield (1996) points out, gendered assumptions about the degree of agency being exercised have traditionally played a part in determining the nature of the response. Here, she maintains, men's unreason has generally been viewed as incorporating agency with the attribution of responsibility. In contrast, women's unreason has tended to be seen as something outside women's control, with agency and responsibility not being foregrounded. Arguably as a result, men's unreason has been subject to more overt forms of control, particularly when mental distress, anguish and unreason have taken a violent form or have resulted in persistent incapacity with regard to expected social performance. Indeed, Gove and Tudor in 1973 and Pleck in 1981 drew attention to gendered roles being oppressive for men and highlighted that the emphasis placed on achievement, on providing for a family and on the expectation that 'men' can hold their own in all situations resulted in the creation of a variety of stressors which affected different men in different ways, with some of these having a very negative effect on mental well-being.

The *Men and Masculinities* literature can be seen to have provided a more nuanced analysis and the considerable work of writers such as Connell (e.g. 2000, 2005) and Hearn (e.g. 2002, 2005) and Pease (2003) locates men within the context of patriarchy and within divisions of class, race, sexuality and other forms of social inequality, whilst at the same time exploring the ways in which patriarchal belief systems can become embedded in men's psyches. As a result, although systemic power imbalances generally work in men's favour, the structures of power operate differentially, with a range of factors combining to influence the extent to which different men can benefit from patriarchy (Hanlon, 2008).

In Chapter 10, we look at the ways in which power imbalances translate into forms of negative discrimination and oppression, and for men as well as for women we maintain that experiences of mental health have to be seen as gendered and as influenced by ethnicity, by socio-economic position, by social class and by the manifestation of entrenched forms of racism. Barn (2008) points out that with regard to discussions about ethnicity in particular, the emphasis placed on exploring aspects associated with cultural relativity (which prioritize the exploration of how mental distress is conceptualized by different cultural groups and how this differs from the mainstream) serves to over-emphasize cultural criteria and to under-emphasize the interconnections between ethnicity, gender and social class. Fernando (2002) maintains that it is important to fully acknowledge the operation of Eurocentric knowledge frameworks and the implicit privileging of westernized conceptualizations of mental health. He asserts:

...if psychiatry is to participate fully in the promotion of mental health, it must break out of its ethnocentrism, free itself of racism and reach out into the world it has so far ignored. In doing so it must recognise certain social realities concerned with power: the economic and military domination of the world by power blocks which identify with white superiority and with values that are largely to do with Western materialism – values that are promoted as being 'modern' and superior to those of so-called traditional societies; the blending of power with racism, both within nations and internationally'; and the involvement of psychiatry with the exercise of power – state power working through psychiatry and personal power of professionals over patients.

(Fernando, 2002: 136–137)

Fernando's (2002) analysis about how power imbalances can operate at a range of intersecting levels provides a backdrop for a discussion about the different experiences of different groups of men in relation to mental health. Although, men have traditionally been under-represented in mental health statistics, the picture has been very different for Irish men, young Black African Caribbean men and Indigenous men in Australia. These groups, which in turn are characterized by heterogeneity rather than homogeneity, appear to experience greater rates of compulsory admission to hospital under mental health legislation than other groups. Explanations for such over-representation emphasize both socially causative and socially constructionist elements. The former draws attention to the historical, as well as for some groups, the ongoing effects of oppression and colonialism, as well as the disproportionate experience of a range of disadvantages associated with low socio-economic status and the social determinants of ill-health generally. The latter focuses on how particular groups can be viewed as posing a threat or a danger and the ways in which they can be discursively construed as 'other'. A range of writers, including Francis (1988), Littlewood (1992), Fernando et al. (1998) and Fernando (2002), have viewed the over-representation of young Black African Caribbean men in psychiatric statistics for schizophrenia, for example, as an indication of the role played by psychiatry in forming part of the social control apparatus. Indigenous men, in Australia particularly, can be seen to have been subject to the interplay of social causational and social constructionist elements and to find themselves disproportionally and negatively represented in all statistics

relating to prison populations, compulsory mental health deten-
tions, as well as alcohol and substance abuse and domestic violence figures. Increasingly, in Australia, as discussed in earlier
chapters, both the Federal as well as the State and Territory governments are recognizing that the historical and social context
for Indigenous health and well-being has to be fully taken into
account and that this forms a necessary pre-requisite for considerations of mental health and mental ill-health (Bland et al.,
2009). As part of this process, the importance of tackling pervasive inequalities associated with socio-economic status, housing,
access to health care, education and employment opportunities
is gradually being taken on board as is the imperative of incorporating spiritual, holistic and cultural understandings of mental
well-being into conceptualizations of mental health. However, it
has to be recognized that all too often, innovative and holistic
initiatives, which emphasize collaboration and participation, sit
side by side with an enduring systemic emphasis on 'top down
responses' which continue both to pathologize and to discrimi-
nate against undervalued groups. The 2007 Northern Territories Intervention in Australia enacted by the Federal Howard-
led National Liberal Coalition serves as a good example here.
Although related to addressing allegations of child sexual abuse
rather than mental health issues, the controlling, non-inclusive
and authoritarian action taken provides an enduring example of
a complex matter being addressed by 'top down', exclusionary
and non-participatory means (Fawcett and Hanlon, 2009b).

In any discussion of men and masculinities, it has also to be
acknowledged that homosexuality was only de-classified from the
Psychiatric Diagnostic and Statistical Manual (version III) as a mental
illness in 1973 and that it remained in the International Statistical Classification of Diseases and Related Health Problems (ICD)
until 1992. This has left a legacy of distrust and fear of both
overt and covert forms of homophobic pathologization. Gay men,
as with other groups of men who have been subject to wide-
ranging discrimination, experience both additional stressors in
terms of prejudicial attitudes and violence, as well as negative
constructions which position them as 'abnormal', 'deviant' and
'perverted'. However, it is notable that gay challenges to such
responses have met with considerable success and have resulted,
within a relatively short period of time, in marked changes to
social attitudes and legislation.

Social determinants of mental ill-health

As we explored in the preceding discussion, social and economic inequalities mediated by the intersection of dimensions
connected with gender, 'race', class and sexuality both create
mental distress as well as affect how some women and men are
viewed and responded to. As we have seen in the United Kingdom, African Caribbean young men are over-represented in the
mental health system, are disproportionately subject by the police
and courts to admission to medium and highly secure facilities
and are unlikely to see the mental health system as being able
to offer supportive assistance (Wall et al., 1999; Sainsbury Centre
for Mental Health, 2002). Similarly, in Australia, Indigenous people are more likely to experience differential responses (ANTAR,
2004). There are also specific issues that can be seen, for example, to affect younger Asian women in the United Kingdom,
where high rates of suicide have been reported (Bhardwaj, 2001;
Wilson, 2001). The World Health Organization is increasingly
acknowledging these inequities, and although not foregrounding
social constructionist factors, they are emphasizing the role that
social determinants play in the arena of mental ill-health (Friedli,
WHO, 2009).

The 2009 WHO Report written by Lynne Friedli states:

> ...levels of mental distress among communities need to be under-
> stood less in terms of individual pathology and more as a response
> to relative deprivation and social injustice, which erode the emo-
> tional, spiritual and intellectual resources essential to psychological
> wellbeing' Friedli.

> (Friedli, WHO, 2009: iii)

According to Sheppard (2002), a close association between mental ill-health and poverty has been demonstrated in studies over
the past half-century. Whilst both men and women may live in
poverty, in the United Kingdom, Australia and the United States,
women have been shown to be more vulnerable to poverty, particularly in relation to single-parent status and as single older
women (Rodgers, 1990; Buck, 1997; Hancock, 2001; Roof, 2001).
Brown and Harris (1978) in research which was groundbreak-
ing at the time found that for poorer women paid employment
acted as a 'protective factor' against the development of depression. However, there have been many social changes since this

landmark study and contemporary challenges for lone parents might well mean more vulnerability to poverty and stress when employment is juggled alongside the availability, cost and quality of child care. Indeed, lone mothers who work full-time have been found to be more susceptible to stress and to poor mental health generally (Brown and Moran, 1997; Baker and North, 1999). Clearly, employment can confer economic, social and psychological benefits on the individual and play an important role in structuring daily life. Although individuals with a history of mental ill-health generally have lower rates of employment, there is evidence that even those who experience long-term and severe mental ill-health can benefit from creative and supported employment opportunities (Evans and Repper, 2000). However, as we discuss in Chapter 10, punitive approaches to fostering employment can have a negative effect and increase the overall levels of stress experienced.

The WHO Report (Freidli, 2009) draws attention to a 'life course' approach to mental health and focuses on how inequalities from conception, early childhood and adolescence can contribute to poor mental health for adults. As discussed in Chapters 4 and 5, we argue against the application of a simplistic cause and effect model, but clearly mental ill-health prevention and mental health promotion programmes can have a significant effect, particularly if these target inequalities and focus on adequate incomes, good housing and quality education. The WHO Report maintains that tackling inequalities across WHO member states is the major challenge and contends that:

> understanding the importance of mental health can help us to think more critically about the limits of economic growth and what wealth can achieve and to promote greater awareness of the benefits of reducing inequalities.

> (Freidli, WHO Report, 2009: v)

The concomitant implications for policy and practice include focusing on the social, cultural and economic conditions that support family life with these encompassing systematically working to reduce child poverty, providing support for parents, strengthening interagency partnerships to reduce violence and sexual abuse and emphasizing the importance of a good work-life balance. There is also a policy and practice emphasis on reducing pervasive inequalities with regard to educational and employment opportunities, on promoting community responses to mental health promotion and mental ill-health prevention and on working to reduce barriers to social contact.

Concluding remarks

In this chapter, we have looked at mental health in relation to adults. As with children and young people, the rising statistics draw attention to a range of influencing factors. These include enduring social inequalities and social determinants as well as aspects which affect how an individual or group is being positioned. The increasing attention directed towards the social determinants of mental health by influential bodies such as the World Health Organization is also serving both to foreground social justice and to operate as a corrective to an over-emphasis on individual pathology. It is also providing a much-needed impetus for governments to spend money on community-orientated responses. It appears apposite to end this chapter with a quote from Friedli and the WHO (2009) Report:

> It has been said that the public mental health equivalent of sewers and clean water are respect and justice. This suggests that important as specific interventions are – in early years, in schools, in the workplace, in neighbourhoods and in primary care – the urgent policy priority is to promote and protect respect and justice – the underlying principles that support mental wellbeing.
>
> (Freidli, WHO, 2009: 41)

In Chapter 7, we turn our attention to older women and men. We examine how older people generally are paradoxically positioned within welfare discourses as 'costs to be managed' and as 'active consumers', and we explore the implications of the contemporary emphasis on areas such as 'risk', 'vulnerability' and 'protection'.

CHAPTER 7

Older Women and Men and Mental Health: Turning Around the Stereotypes

As we have seen throughout this book, health, which includes mental health and well-being, can be seen to be a multidimensional and holistic concept which incorporates a range of factors. These clearly relate to socio-economic influences, life course outcomes and quality of life issues. In addition, older women and men generally have to contend with additional matters which can include the deaths of contemporaries and changing life patterns. These, in turn, can be affected by levels of social and financial security and the accessibility of community and family support. Older people can also fear both increasing incapacity and perceived lack of capacity which can result in a loss of control over what happens to them.

In tandem with the statistics relating to children, young people and adults, it appears that the number of older people diagnosed with mental health problems in the community is growing. In the context of the United Kingdom, Manthorpe and Iliffe (2005) have highlighted that depression affects one in five older people living in the community and two in five living in residential homes. The National Institute for Clinical Excellence (UK) (2004) in the United Kingdom has also estimated that dementia affects 5 per cent of people over the age of 65 and 20 per cent of those over 80. This equates to 1.2 per cent of the population at any one time. As discussed in previous chapters, the reasons for this increase in mental health diagnoses can variously be attributed to a combination of demographic trends, to an increasing number of problems being experienced by older people, as well as to more older people being identified, or at times possibly constructed as, experiencing mental ill-health. In this chapter, we will explore formulations of mental health as they affect older people. As part of this process, we will examine the importance of place, how older people are positioned in relation to mental health issues and welfare discourses generally and the ways in which considerations of 'risk' and safety can conflict with self-determined views about emotional well-being.

Place and position

Characteristics of place can be seen to influence the health and well-being of individuals and populations, and ageing can be regarded as being 'emplaced' within individual, community and wider socio-economic contexts (Milne et al., 2007; Fawcett, 2008). Age and the implications of ageing are conceptualized differently within different cultural situations and factors such as respect, the valuing of experience and the sense of an individual being linked to a specific place and a social space can have a profound influence on mental health and well-being.

Historically as well, Biggs and Powell (2001) argue that different discourses of welfare have positioned older people in a number of ways, inevitably influencing experiences and perceptions. Employing a genealogical approach derived from Foucault, which both traces and critically interrogates historical pathways that have contributed to contemporary circumstances, they equate the consolidation of social welfare systems after the Second World War with the emplacement of what has continued to be a pervasive ambiguity about old age and older people. As a result, in the immediate post-war period, whilst on the one hand older adults were portrayed as heroic survivors, on the other hand their social welfare needs were placed at the end of a considerable queue. This juxtaposition has continued through both the marketization of social welfare and the emergence of the social investment state. Biggs and Powell (2001) draw parallels between this negative social welfare inference and dominant themes in the medicalized literature on ageing, which is heavily influenced by an inference on decline and maintenance. They also regard psychological perspectives, particularly those derived from psychoanalysis, to have had a pathologizing influence. They state:

> Social Welfare came to colonize the meaning given to old age in the popular imagination, and the Welfare State came to characterize the place, the discourse, in relationship to which ageing identities have come to be formed, a master-narrative of decline, a recognition of respect and stigma of lost personal control.
>
> (Biggs and Powell, 2001: 10)

As this analysis has a bearing on issues relating to older people and mental health, we will explore the arguments in greater detail.

Looking first at the social welfare discourse of marketization which came to the fore during the Thatcher/Reagan era in the West, it is clear that these policies continued to perpetuate ambiguity. Accordingly, the emphasis on 'case' and 'care' management and the implementation of new managerialist policies in human service organizations can be seen to have promoted a change in emphasis from general social welfare to a heightened focus on surveillance and control. The policies underpinning marketization also brought to the fore the concept of 'risk' as a means of privatizing and individualizing social ills, rolling back universally orientated forms of support and putting in place gatekeeping mechanisms to direct services, as discussed in Chapter 5, towards risk-managing individuals along ascribed trajectories. This not only reframed service eligibility but also reforged the notion of the importance of protection for older people. As a result, assessing 'capacity' both in terms of mental and physical capability came to dominate service provision together with a perceived need to protect older people from various forms of elder abuse or neglect. However, notwithstanding the realities of gatekeeping mechanisms, capped funding thresholds and risk assessments, this social welfare perspective also positioned older people as active consumers newly able to exercise choice and autonomy in an era of 'needs led' provision.

With regard to 'third-way' perspectives and the emphasis placed on a social investment state by the Labour Government in the United Kingdom when it came to power in 1997, older people's lack of fit with narratives of progress and investment for the future in terms of work and contribution towards a taxation base have continued to fuel ambiguity. It also contributed to the contradictory portrayal of older people generally as both a 'drain on the economy' and a cost which has to be carefully managed, and as 'active citizens' within a social inclusion agenda. The 'risk' discourse also continues apace, with manifestations of 'risk' for older people being continually extended into a wider range of areas including, as Biggs and Powell point out:

> The risk of giving in to an ageing body, the risk of thereby being excluded from one's retirement community, the risk of being too poor to maintain a consumer lifestyle, the risk of being excluded from participation through incapacity that has been externally assessed, the risk of being abused, the risk of control being taken out of one's hands, the risk of tokenism in partnership, and so on.
>
> (Biggs and Powell, 2001: 16)

In the field of mental health, widely held assumptions and value judgements resulting from the impact of these various welfare discourses can serve to influence responses and can lead to older people's experiences and self-expressed needs being insufficiently valued. Older people tend frequently to be referred to as comprising an homogenized group, with ambiguity and negativity featuring strongly. As a result, older people have to regularly contend with being referred to as a 'burden to medical services'. Exhortations to be 'active consumers' or 'active citizens' can serve to increase personal responsibility for not becoming ill or distressed and the negative subject positions afforded to groups or individuals who are unable to exercise such personal and social responsibility can serve to restrict the opportunities available for constructive and positive self-positioning. This can clearly influence an individual's sense of well-being and their mental health (Fawcett and Reynolds, 2010).

Beddoe and Maidment (2009) re-emphasize the point made above and maintain that Western society's current obsession with risk has created a new category of people who are seen to be 'at risk' and as a result to exist in a permanent condition of vulnerability. As a consequence, individual identities can be subsumed within perceived vulnerabilities, and older people experiencing any form of mental distress or confusion tend to quickly be categorized and referred to as 'the vulnerable'. The acceptance of this terminology within policy and practice militates against an older person being seen to have a tangible presence and as having a significant contribution to make to their family and community. Fawcett (2009) interrogates understandings of 'vulnerability' so often associated with older people. She notes that the purpose of identification and assessment as a vulnerable adult is to provide appropriate support and to guard against harm, but she emphasizes that this dominant interpretation is also one where perceived weaknesses rather than strengths can so easily dominate and where dependency and passivity prevail over self-determination and autonomy. Grenier (2004), on the basis of a study carried out with older women, also questions what she refers to as organizationally reductionist assessments of risk and frailty. She points to these practices ignoring holistic concepts of well-being and those aspects regarded by older women as particularly important. In relation to the latter, Grenier (2004) found that these included a day-to-day acceptance of uncertainty and the prioritization of individualized matters which the women saw as important to them in the context of their daily lives.

Human rights and capacity

Human rights issues have always featured significantly in relation to mental health. However, as Spandler and Carlton (2009) argue, human rights legislation can fail to protect those with a diagnosis of mental illness. This is because human rights legislation can place mental illness outside the parameters of human experience and can prioritize exceptionalist rather than universalist criteria. Spandler and Carlton (2009) highlight that human rights legislation not only tends to defer to medical authority, but that mental health legislation always 'trumps' the enactment of human rights legislation.

When considering issues relating to human rights and mental health, as highlighted earlier, judgements about 'capacity' have a particular and contemporary relevance for older people. The Mental Capacity Act (2005) in the United Kingdom starts off from the assumption of capacity, with lack of capacity having to be proved on a case-by-case basis. This legislation is regarded as progressive because it enables people to make advance decisions, to appoint proxy decision-makers with lasting power of attorney and to incorporate the operation of the Mental Capacity Advocate

Service. This latter body provides advocacy services for those assessed as lacking capacity who do not have friends or family members. This Act has also introduced additional criminal offences to further protect those deemed to lack capacity from wilful neglect or ill-treatment. In Australia, although legislation varies from state to state, again decisions about incapacity are made on an individualized basis (Bennett and Hallen, 2005), with Guardianship Tribunals playing a dominant role. However, in both countries considerable weight is placed on expert opinion and proof of incapacity for an older person often rests on a standardized assessment of cognitive functioning by a psychiatrist or psycho-geriatrician. Given that such assessments are often made within a context where professionals are exhorted to prioritize the physical safety of the older person and the eradication of risk over self-determination, the potential for judgements about incapacity overruling those emphasizing capacity is considerable.

Community mental health

Throughout this book, we have promoted the further development of community-orientated approaches to mental health. Manthorpe and Iliffe (2005) argue for an investment in people that facilitates the prevention or pre-emption of mental health problems and which supports measures that include reducing social isolation, creating supportive environments, addressing financial difficulties and activating social befriending schemes. Looking specifically at older peoples' experiences of depression, they maintain that professionals should focus on social orientations that highlight the amelioration of problems, rather than a unidimensional, medically orientated focus on a 'cure'. As part of this process, they emphasize the importance of continually weaving a network of support. In this context, as we have previously highlighted, strengths-based approaches have a particular role to play in reframing experiences and addressing challenges (Fawcett and Reynolds, 2009).

Community-orientated responses place emphasis on 'wellness' and on health promotion and ill-health prevention programmes which prioritize exercise and healthy eating (Friedli WHO, 2009). Leonard and Johansson (2008) draw from research carried out by Onyx and Warburton (2003), to point to the strong link which has been established between social networks and healthy ageing, particularly in relation to the connections forged between volunteering and social capital with regard to the maintenance of health and psychological well-being into old age. Taking these findings on board, they compare the policies and practices developed for engaging older people in community life in both Sweden and Australia. Their findings show that in Australia, as a result of services being provided and funded by three levels of government as well as by third sector or NGOs, the associated emphasis on competition, short-term funding and constant contract renewal promotes confusion and lack of confidence. Accordingly, the complicated and fragmented nature of age care services operates as a barrier to community involvement. They also draw attention to the blocks to active engagement in the community which have been brought about by 'new managerialist' practices and which have influenced both access to, as well as the operation of, services, restricting both flexibility and inclusivity. These barriers, they maintain, are additionally reinforced by ageist attitudes in which the capacity of people to contribute is perceived as declining with age. They also highlight how small amounts of assistance in areas such as house cleaning, garden maintenance, telephone and internet access, interactive day centres, lunch clubs, general communication links and transport can promote effective community contributions which bring with them a range of associated benefits.

With regard to ageing and the involvement of older people in building social capacity, the situation in Sweden highlights a different range of issues. The differences can be associated with older people in Sweden having been protected by a range of welfare measures, particularly those focusing on pensions and disability. There is also a different volunteering pattern with greater emphasis being placed on volunteering in organizations which promote the interests of their members, such as trade unions and those involved in sporting, recreational or cultural activities, rather than in welfare agencies. However, Leonard and Johansson (2008) suggest that the emphasis on well-resourced welfare services in Sweden, although currently subject to financial review, has served to promote a bureaucratic rather than a community management model. They argue that a community management model would provide older people with more opportunities to use their knowledge and skills and would result in greater innovation. This could include running community forums with input from a range of people to inform new directions for social services in the municipality or the establishment of local committees to identify local priorities.

Social supports

We maintain that the generation and provision of a variety of forms of community and social support can play a pivotal role in engaging those who are struggling with mental health difficulties or those who have received a diagnosis of mental illness. Although there are discrepancies relating to the ways in which social support is both defined and measured, the importance, as well as the protective effects of social support on health and mental health factors, can be continually re-emphasized. Howie et al. (2004), for example, draw attention to how the recognition of older people's skills through purposeful activities in health services or community environments can support and maintain personal and social identities and can significantly contribute to experiences of well-being and adaptation to life events.

In relation to older people who are experiencing increasing impairments, it is also becoming clear that the psycho-social support obtained through a range of 'day-club' provision can significantly influence mental health and well-being. A study carried out by Tse and Howie (2005), for example, highlights the importance for participants of companionship and the positive benefits of group activities. They emphasize how participants value 'keeping occupied', 'having something to look forward to' and activities which 'keep our brains working'. They also draw attention to many club members finding long periods at home to be unstimulating, distressing and boring, with many who experience difficulty going out on their own describing their home as 'a trap'. Fawcett (2011) also draws attention to the significance of 'mixed roles' with 'day-club' participants attending at different times as both volunteers and club members.

Seeman et al. (2002) tested the hypothesis that social experiences affect a range of biological systems using the concept of cumulative biological risk or allostatic load. They collected data from two cohorts – one comprising older people in the 70–79 age range, the other focusing on those in the 50–59-year age group. Allostatic load was assessed using identical protocols in the two cohorts. Their finding supported their hypothesis that positive social experiences are associated with lower allostatic loads and that social experiences affect a range of biological systems which positively influence a variety of health and mental health outcomes.

Studies carried out by House, Robbins and Metzner (1982) and Kaplan (1988) have also demonstrated the positive effects of psycho-social support systems for older men and women experiencing increasing impairments. Lyyra and Heikkinen (2006), in a study which examined the relationship between social supports, health and mental health for those with an average age of 80, also found that the risk of death was almost 2.5 times higher for women who received infrequent assurances of worth, lacked emotional closeness and a sense of belonging, and had few opportunities to demonstrate affection for others.

Clearly, the success of 'day clubs' is influenced by the availability of resources as well as by members' participation in the planning and organization of activities. However, they can generate a sense of collectivism which can be experienced as a means of socializing individual concerns and strengths. They can also serve to build social capacity, blurring the boundaries between volunteering and participation and between day centre engagement and community involvement. In this respect, Fawcett (2011) found in her study that 'day clubs' not only fostered a sense of well-being but that they also encouraged the undertaking of additional activities and engagement with both family and community networks outside the club.

'Day clubs' can be seen as one community-orientated option which promotes greater community and social engagement. However, in relation to any kind of provision, there can be pitfalls, particularly if one course of action or set of operating principles is subject to particular prioritization. Roulstone and Morgan (2009) highlight the danger of a particular policy platform being used to unilaterally shape services. They point to a greater emphasis on choice and self-determination in policy agendas sounding like a 'good thing' but highlight the dangers of this resulting in a renewed emphasis on individualized forms of provision with the concomitant outcome of enforced individualism and isolation. They emphasize the importance of responding to diversity and recognizing that older people want different things. They stress the need to prevent ideological positions, which are often promoted as bringing about major improvements for consumers, being allowed to increase rigidity and inflexibility.

The 'well-being' agenda

As we saw earlier in this chapter, well-being, as a concept and as a 'state of being', is re-gaining currency in relation to discourses of old age and mental health. As a concept, it relates both to the ways in which a government can promote the well-being of its citizens as well as to a citizens' responsibility, to themselves and to their community and society, to promote their own well-being. It is associated with a reduction of expenditure on health care and to a decline in dangerous pursuits such as smoking, drinking heavily and eating badly. In current policy jargon, it can be described as a 'win, win' situation. However, there are pitfalls. Not least, to re-iterate the point made earlier, well-being as a 'state of being' can easily become the responsibility of the citizen or older person. As a result, the effect of significant social and economic barriers to good mental health can be minimized and emphasis placed instead on the pathology of the individual. This can easily result in additional stigmatization for those whose social and economic situation places them at a disadvantage and can serve to direct attention away from the social determinants of mental distress and poor mental health.

Edwards and Imrie (2008) argue that the promotion of well-being, in its current form, is unlikely to benefit older people experiencing mental distress or ill-health. They maintain that the individualizing emphasis on personality and character traits and the concomitant downplaying of social and structural forces allows governments to highlight capacity-building manoeuvres and self-help whilst at the same time reducing expenditure on social infrastructures. There is clearly something of a paradox here in that community responses are being promoted as part of a personalizing emphasis on well-being. Perhaps, a way forward is to reframe the agenda and to emphasize collective responsibility for well-being, rather than to allow the pathologization of 'states of being' which fall short of what could so easily become an idealized standard. Well-being has a positive currency, particularly in relation to older people and mental health and the devaluing of this term has wide-ranging implications.

Considerations of dementia

There can be a tendency for mental health problems experienced in later life to be linked with forms of dementia. Such associations can foster simplistic categorization processes and serve to obscure a wide range of experiences, expectations and service requirements (Fawcett and Reynolds, 2009). However, even when a diagnosis of dementia has been obtained, there are perspectives which counter a traditional emphasis on loss, lack and increasing deficiency. Social model understanding of mental health, for example, has been applied to the broad field of dementia and has focused on eradicating images of dementia as a 'living death' and as the loss of personhood (Kitwood, 1997; Hughes et al., 2006; Hughes, 2011). Sabat (2002) reconstructs dementia and maintains that personal identity, understood in terms of obligations, experiences, responsibilities and beliefs about physical and mental attributes, continues to be both preserved and continually interwoven into an individual's ongoing life story or narrative. He argues that we all need the co-operation of others to re-inforce our sense of self, but that all too often a diagnosis of dementia erodes this co-operation and results in a negative reconstruction of the individual. This perspective does not dismiss biological changes, but rather focuses on the maintenance of identity through constructive social support and re-inforcement. It reconfigures the ageing process to foreground strengths and positive aspects rather than negative factors associated with loss and decline.

Stanley and Manthorpe (2008) also draw attention to the importance of 'best interest' decisions not being based on unjustified assumptions. Drawing from Koppelman (2002), they highlight that the views and interests of both the 'previous self' as well as the 'present self' of a person with dementia should be taken into account. In this, they maintain that a detailed knowledge of the wishes, feelings, beliefs and values of the person has to counterbalance the views, orientation and possible prejudices of the person making a decision on their behalf. By paying attention to a person's history and considering the choices they would be likely to have made, they assert that individual personhood can be upheld and subjective interests can be acknowledged.

Concluding remarks

To say that we all look forward to old age is to state the obvious as well as to engage in a play on words which highlights a prevailing fear of becoming old. Ageing is a process which we can deny, attempt to hide or embrace as part of life's experiential tapestry. Our responses will shape our adaptability and affect how we manage change. For some, the pressures will become too much, for others, attempts to influence how we are seen by our contemporaries and by members of other generations will meet with varying amounts of success. We can hope that a focus on what we can do will outway emphasis being placed on what we cannot do. We can hope that whatever happens to us our lives will retain meaning, through our own eyes as well as through those of significant others. We can also hope that we are not immobilized by fixed interpretations and disabling constructions and that account is taken of diverse perspectives and responses. We also, in terms of the contributions we can make, have a crucial role to play in turning around the stereotypes.

In Chapter 8, we direct a critical lens towards the concept of 'dual diagnosis'. We appraise clinical definitions and review social implications. Throughout, we highlight the relevance of this discussion for mental health across the lifespan and we draw attention to pertinent areas.

PART III

Mental Health Landscapes

CHAPTER 8

The Case of Dual Diagnosis

The concept of 'dual diagnosis' has gained considerable currency within clinical psychiatric practice in Western nations, particularly in Australia, over recent years. In this chapter, we both recognize the operational identity that 'dual diagnosis' has acquired in the current climate and also scrutinize what can be regarded as an expansion of psychiatric diagnostic criteria into territory which is both social and marginalized. We therefore explore definitional issues as well as consider the overall implications of this framework. As part of this process, we examine the tensions that arise in relation to service user or consumer perspectives and the challenges posed for socially orientated understandings of mental health.

The clinical identity of dual diagnosis

Matters of definition

Definitions of the term 'dual diagnosis' can be seen to vary between those which focus specifically on psychiatric classification and those which emphasize a strong social component. White et al. (2005) from within clinical practice define it as 'a co-morbidity referring to the presence of at least two distinct and separate disabilities or pathologies in the same individual' (White et al., 2005: 396). However, the University of Queensland (2002) describes adults with a 'dual diagnosis' as a non-homogenous population who when considered together form a very diverse group. They maintain that this heterogeneity incorporates complex social factors which render the provision of assistance challenging and as non-amenable to standardization. However, in most practice settings, the term 'dual diagnosis' is used as a form of psychiatric categorization which generally refers to a diagnosed mental illness co-existing with a recognized form of substance abuse. The extent to which social factors are acknowledged as part of a biopsychosocial approach, which is part of the medicalized spectrum, but at the opposite end to a physical or biological approach, varies from setting to setting.

In terms of the production of standardized criteria, as highlighted in previous chapters, the Diagnostic and Statistical Manual of Disorders (DSM-IV and DSM-V) is the product of the American Psychiatric Association (2000, 2013) and is used worldwide as a means of classifying mental disorders or illnesses. As discussed in Chapter 2, the centrality afforded to diagnoses within psychiatric practice and the part played in this by the reification of diagnostic tools such as the DSM, in all of its versions, have been subject to much criticism (Blashfield, 1996; Boyle, 2000; Lewis, 2006). Although from within the American Psychological Association it is acknowledged that 'the concept of mental disorder like many other concepts in medicine and science lacks a consistent operational definition that covers all situations' (DSM IV, 2000: xxx), the classifications are afforded significant clinical authenticity and authority. Within the DSMs generally, there is a focus on identifying prevailing symptoms and reviewing these in relation to other dimensions or axes to confirm the diagnosis. These dimensions or axes incorporate the noting of current and previous physical disorders, ascertaining the severity of the current symptoms, assessing 'the patient's' current level of functioning and assessing the highest level of functioning which 'the patient' has achieved during the course of the year. This review can also include a biopsychosocial emphasis.

In relation to these classificatory systems, substance abuse or substance use disorder is defined as a persistent maladaptive pattern of behaviour which results in significant adverse consequences. Within clinical practice, substance use disorder tends to be diagnosed when there is repeated failure to fulfil major role obligations, when there is repeated use of a substance in situations where it is physically hazardous and when substance use leads to recurrent social and interpersonal problems. Examples of failure to fulfil major role obligations may include neglect of children, poor work performance, recurrent hangovers and, for young people, absences or suspensions from school. Substance abuse disorders also tend to be clinically diagnosed if an individual continues to use substances despite a history of persistent or recurrent ill-effects and/or when there can be seen to be a clear pattern with an individual moving repeatedly from displaying apparent tolerance, making numerous attempts at withdrawal and displaying harmful physical effects.

The relevance of the clinical concept

The prevalence of the term 'dual diagnosis', involving a combination of diagnosed mental illness and substance abuse, varies across different countries and cultures. This relates to the different ways that cultures perceive and conceptualize mental distress, mental illness and substance abuse and the relevance of this diagnosis for different settings. In relation to an association between substance abuse, mental illness and suicide, research by Xiao et al. (2008), for example, suggests that in Asian countries socio-cultural stressors are a greater indicator of suicide than diagnosed mental illness and substance use disorders. They also highlight that primary health care in many Asian countries does not focus on clinical diagnoses. This relates both to differing conceptualizations of mental ill-health as well as to resource constraints which militate against the wide-scale adoption of Western frames of reference. In the United States and many parts of Europe, including the United Kingdom, suicide risk which involves substance abuse, is identified as a mental health issue. This aspect, together with a continued emphasis on the importance of a classificatory framework, has resulted in the concept of 'dual diagnosis' acquiring a wide-ranging currency (Flaskenid, 1992; Tellias, 2001).

In terms of the clinical associations which can be made between substance abuse and diagnosed mental illness, Kessler et al. (1994) conducted a National Co-morbidity Survey in the United States. This study examined the extent of co-morbidity between substance use and mental illness. The survey found that 78 per cent of men and 86 per cent of women with alcohol dependence also had a diagnosed mental illness, with this including personality disorders. It further identified that every fourth individual admitted to a mental health inpatient facility/hospital in the United States was abusing an illegal substance and that one in three was abusing alcohol. Research by Tellias (2001) claims that approximately 20 per cent of the adult population in the United States experience some form of substance use disorder and that approximately 60 per cent of individuals with a diagnosis of schizophrenia are also dependent on at least one other substance. Although the definition of substance abuse includes excessive use of alcohol, it is notable that most research into substance abuse focuses on illegal drug taking. In comparison, very little research has been carried out into the overuse of prescription medication and the relationship between this and mental ill-health.

The National Drug and Alcohol Research Centre (Mattick et al., 1998) conducted research on a sample of 270 methadone maintenance consumers from three separate clinics (non-government) in Sydney, Australia, and found significantly higher lifetime rates of clinically recognized depression (30%), social phobia (40%) and anti-social personality (42%) in comparison to the general population. Work completed by New South Wales Health (2000), in Australia, reported links between mental illness and increased rates of substance use disorders. For example, it found associations between clinically recognized mood disorders and alcohol and stimulant abuse; between personality disorders, particularly anti-social and borderline personality disorders and alcohol and polysubstance abuse; between anxiety disorder and alcohol and benzodiazepines abuse; between post-traumatic stress disorder and alcohol and cannabis abuse; between eating disorders and alcohol and stimulant abuse; and between conduct disorders and alcohol and polysubstance abuse.

SANE, Australia (2007), has expressed concern about the lack of facilities for those clinically identified as having a 'dual diagnosis'. They acknowledge that while the scale of this form of diagnosis in Australia varies, existing research indicates that approximately

- 25 per cent of people diagnosed with anxiety disorders, affective disorders and substance use disorders have also been diagnosed with another mental health disorder.
- 64 per cent of psychiatric in-patients may have a current or previous drug use problem.
- 75 per cent of people with alcohol and substance use problems may have a clinically recognized form of illness.

- 90 per cent of males diagnosed with schizophrenia may have a substance use problem.

They highlight that these figures suggest that people with a diagnosis of mental illness are more likely to have a substance use disorder than people without a diagnosed mental illness and vice versa. However, it also has to be stated that those with a diagnosis of mental illness are also more likely to have their behaviour monitored with additional issues being recorded.

External perceptions

SANE, Australia (2007), states that individuals with diagnosed mental illnesses and substance use disorders are more likely to have experienced

- considerable social problems,
- severe symptoms of a mental health disorder/illness with a high likelihood of recurrence,
- fluctuating emotional states,
- hospitalization or frequent visits to emergency departments,
- alienation and a lack of support from family and friends,
- homelessness or moving frequently from one place of residence to another,
- being perceived as not cooperating with health care providers.

SANE, Australia (2007), maintains that people with a 'dual diagnosis' appreciate and respond well to programmes that address both mental health issues as well as those relating to substance abuse. However, they acknowledge that it is hard to find professionals who are skilled in working with individuals who have been subject to 'dual diagnoses'. They state that the number of workers trained to work in this field is slowly increasing but that the services for mental health and substance use disorders generally do not overlap. As a result, silos often prevail and professionals in one field are not necessarily knowledgeable about issues in the other.

At this point, it is useful to look at four models of service provision which have been used by New South Wales Health (2000) in Australia in response to 'dual diagnosis' as these draw attention to current system responses. These models can be referred to as

(1) The prevention model
(2) The sequential model
(3) The parallel model
(4) The integrated model

The prevention model

Drawing from research carried out by Mrazek and Haggerty (1994) and Kenny et al. (2006), New South Wales Health (2000) has directed attention towards adolescent populations (particularly those in the 15-year-old age group). This is because young people, particularly boys, are seen as being most at risk of attempting or committing suicide as a result of life changes, emotional upheaval, excessive alcohol consumption, binge drinking and experimentation with drugs and substances generally. As a result educational programmes in schools have been promoted as one strategy to assist in preventing substance abuse through the promotion of self-care, the building of individual strengths and by increasing the capacity of young people to cope and manage life issues and/or stressors. Cappo (2006) reinforces the importance of promoting a more holistic model of support and service delivery and highlights that this needs to take into account all aspects of an individual's life.

The sequential model

The sequential model is referred to by New South Wales Health (2000) as a clinical model of treatment which promotes the delivery of mental health and drug and alcohol services from different spheres. For example, an individual may be treated by one service/system (mental health or drug and alcohol) and then subsequently by the other. The order in which the diagnosed disorders are treated may vary depending on the professional's view of which emerged first or whether it is determined that drug and alcohol or mental health treatment must be given priority. An example of this is abstinence from drug and alcohol use prior to commencing treatment for a diagnosed mental illness. Mental Health America (2008) argues that whilst treatment for both problems simultaneously is ideal, sequential treatment is a helpful first step if someone, who is using substances, detoxes, and then engages in dual treatment programmes.

The parallel model

Ridgely et al. (1990) promote the parallel model which involves the simultaneous involvement of an individual with a 'dual diagnosis' in both mental health and drug and alcohol services to enable the treatment of both diagnoses at the same time. The Revised National Standards for Mental Health Services (Commonwealth Department of Health and Ageing, 2010) and the National Practice Standards for the Mental Health Workforce in Australia (Commonwealth Department of Health and Ageing, 2002) focus on the promotion of comprehensive and co-ordinated services for consumers and their families. As pointed out by the Mental Health Council of Australia (2005), there is still some way to go in terms of meeting this aim, and they draw attention to resource and service constraints failing to support innovation and integration. They also highlight that multi-agency and multi-disciplinary working, whilst encouraged at one level, is not systemically supported at another, and that it is often left to individuals, rather than professionals, to maintain contact with both agencies. However, the emphasis placed by The Revised National Standards for Mental Health Services (Commonwealth Department of Health and Ageing, 2010) on interagency liaison, planning and co-ordination does, at the very least, serve to continue to direct attention towards this area.

The integrated model

Minkoff (1989) states that the development of an integrated model represents best practice in the case of an individual experiencing a 'dual diagnosis' of mental illness and substance use disorder. New South Wales Health (2000) describes integrated treatment as the development of clinical treatment teams with practitioners who are cross-trained in both mental health and drug and alcohol specialities. Service delivery includes linkage into specific treatment programmes, close monitoring, as well as assertive follow-up. Drake et al. (1997) reported that this integrated service model has resulted in reduced substance use, reduced hospitalization and in consumers obtaining greater stability in terms of accommodation. This is supported by Crawford (2007) who states that the integrated model offers better outcomes for this population and is far superior to parallel treatment. Proponents argue that this results from practitioners considering the relationship between substance use disorders and mental illnesses and how the interaction of the two can be directly addressed and management staged according to an individual's needs and readiness for change. However, Hall (1996) suggests that there is the potential for services which are established to provide integrated provision to implement entry criteria which may limit or exclude some individuals assessed as having extensive needs.

Integrated treatment has significant funding implications as additional resources are often required and/or existing resources have to be rearranged and shifted into this area. Given such resource implications, Hall (1997) and Reis (1992) suggest a collaborative model of intervention including joint assessments, co-case management and cross-service consultations with systematic screening of mental health service users/consumers for substance use disorders, and drug and alcohol service users/consumers for mental illnesses. Hall (1997) and Reis (1992) maintain that this resembles a cross between parallel and integrated forms of treatment and that this can be more cost and clinically effective as it utilizes existing service structures and operations. They also point to the importance of educational programmes for practitioners with clear guidelines for interagency and multi-disciplinary partnerships being developed and implemented.

Dual diagnosis: social dimensions

Challenging reductionism

It is clear from the above discussion that 'dual diagnosis' is a clinical formulation designed both to categorize and to facilitate service-orientated responses to people who are experiencing difficulties in a number of areas of their lives. However, the ongoing identification of underlying social factors again raises the issue of the increased medicalization of social issues, and it is notable that Jukes and McLaughlin (2005), in their review of the international literature, emphasize that individuals with diagnosed mental illnesses and substance use disorders tend not to respond well to clinical forms of treatment and that they experience poorer outcomes overall. They state that as a result those with a 'dual diagnosis' tend to be subject to increased rates of hospitalization and incarceration, are more likely to experience homelessness, unemployment and poverty and are at higher risk of suicide. Jukes and McLaughlin (2005) recognize that many individuals who are struggling to keep their lives together either try to access health services or are brought to the attention of health services. However, as highlighted in the preceding section, health services generally tend to be unable to cope with this diverse population and lack the flexibility and resources to provide integrated forms of support. Despite the increasing identification of 'dual diagnosis' in clinical settings, Jukes and McLaughlin (2005) state that generally professional knowledge about this condition is limited and that this can be frustrating for those who seek help. They suggest that health care providers often blame the individual for being difficult and unresponsive to treatment, rather than questioning whether the health care system is failing to provide appropriate services. They also draw attention to situations where individuals are shunted between mental health and drug and alcohol services with neither acknowledging responsibility. Cappo comments:

> People with a dual diagnosis, are in effect, a kind of mental health underclass. They find that their needs are not severe enough to meet the criteria of any single agency. For example, they may have mild ideas of suspicion but may not be clearly psychotic. They may have been to prison but not long enough to be followed up by probation. They may have been squatting with friends, but not technically homeless. There may be no clear reason why social services should allocate a social worker. As a result, they have a dreadful quality of life, even though they may have six or seven major problems, they may receive either no help, or just bits and bobs of help without clear co-ordination.
>
> (Cappo, 2006: 6)

Clearly, the concept of 'dual diagnosis' serves to bring into the spotlight a diverse group for whom there is little support for those who want it. However, the question of whether increased medical categorization helps or hinders progress towards increased forms of support has to be posed. On the one hand, as a 'health' issue, there are resources and protocols and government policy documents continue to emphasize the principles of person-centred support, 'joined up' responses and integrated services. Although there is some way to go in practice, there is clearly a map, dotted with directional signposts. The concept of 'dual diagnosis' also serves to clinically encapsulate those who are deemed a danger to others as well as to themselves and to sanction the taking of appropriate action. However, as we have highlighted in this book and as has been evident in a discussion of the issues in this chapter so far, clinical diagnoses can bring with them the diagnostic reduction of personhood, the devaluing of experiential knowledge and the subjection of an individual to a disorientating combination of mandated treatment and social neglect.

The models discussed earlier focus attention on a range of responses that can be generated by the concept of 'dual diagnosis'. The 'prevention model' in particular emphasizes the important role that can be played by schools and community groups in relation to mental health promotion and mental ill-health prevention. However, the models overall clearly have a strong clinical focus. In relation to young people in particular, whilst this form of provision is valued by some, as pointed out in Chapter 5, many young people often find formal interventions intimidating, overly controlling, paternalistic and as not acknowledging their strengths, nor focusing on their understanding of problem areas and accompanying issues. Kenny et al. (2006) argue in relation to young people (although their arguments have a wider relevance) that consumer involvement is imperative. They maintain that attention needs to be paid to inclusivity and to the effects of power imbalances within clinical settings. They argue for a more socially orientated approach where consumer participation is seen as a pre-requisite for longer term cultural and systemic change. As part of this process the full acknowledgement of experiential knowledge and 'lived experience' is regarded as essential with this going hand in hand with resourced consumer participation in service design, service implementation and service delivery.

In Chapters 1, 2, and 5 we have discussed the importance of context, and at this point it is useful to look again at the relevance of context in relation to psychiatric diagnoses. As highlighted, Bracken and Thomas (2005), both practising psychiatrists, maintain that contextual issues have to be 'centre stage'. They argue that these dimensions of human reality have been pushed back to the edge of our understanding of mental states in particular manifestations of distress and as a consequence have been side lined and marginalized. This can be seen to result in psychiatric classifications having at their core an inherent paradox. The rationale is to return an individual to their pre-illness state or to improve levels of functioning, but reducing lived experiences to a small number of common symptoms, to treat these and to measure success in terms of symptom alleviation not only results in problems being externally identified, but also to success being externally determined. As a result, we argue that the marginalization of these aspects by the processes embedded in the concept of 'dual diagnosis' can serve to pose serious questions about ethical viability as well as about human rights.

The social model of disability as developed by Oliver (1990, 1996, 2006), Shakespeare (1994, 1999), Morris (1993, 1996) and many others challenges the categorization of individuals on the basis of identified impairments or diagnosed conditions and celebrates instead their personhood. Disability is not regarded as an individual issue, but as one created as a result of negative attitudes, physical constraints and social discrimination. Accordingly, an individual is not disabled by an individual impairment or a diagnosed condition, but by negative attitudes, discriminatory value judgements, assumptions about the need for 'care and control' and by pervasive economic, social and political barriers. This perspective strongly critiques the classification and categorization of individuals and focuses instead on challenging medicalizing and institutionalizing constraints. As a result, this understanding is completely at odds with the notion of 'dual diagnosis' and serves as an effective counterpoint to it.

Concluding remarks

'Dual diagnosis' as a concept and as a form of clinical classification is gaining in popularity as a means of identifying problems and formulating responses. This chapter has served both to foreground the underpinning rationales and to draw attention to the limitations of this approach for the lived experiences of those often relegated to the margins. Critiques of standardized provision and accepted practices serve to open up the mental health landscape to more expansive scrutiny and to draw attention to complexity, to the constraints of regularization and to the implications of widening a service user/consumer and professional divide rather than reducing it.

We argue that as many countries focus on reviewing their mental health services, the utility of embracing broader conceptualizations of mental health, the importance of active consumer/service user participation in service planning and delivery, and the imperative of developing innovative and integrated approaches have to be taken on board.

In Chapter 9, we continue this critical yet constructive stance as we consider the concept of 'care' and the identification of family members and others as 'carers'. We look at constructions of 'caring' as well as narratives from those who have chosen to become or who have found themselves occupying this 'upside/down' terrain.

CHAPTER 9

The Upside/Down of Caring: Families in Mental Health

The terminology that surrounds caring relationships and the roles occupied by those who take on or who are ascribed the role of 'carer' can be seen as both descriptive and constructive. 'Caring' can describe what a person does as well as draw attention to a concept which is given meaning through policy documents, practice directives and as a result of a variety of interactions between family members. Caring within families can refer either singly or collectively at different points in time to the presence or absence of emotional ties, to notions of duty that members have for each other and to the provision of a range of forms of support or assistance. 'Caring' can also imply the operation of power imbalances and carry with it the assumption that certain members are more competent than others. In this chapter, we review 'caring' in the context of mental health, mental distress and illness, and we explore a number of diverse perspectives, drawing from individualized as well as socially orientated understandings of mental health.

'Caring' constructions

As Brechin states, 'Caring, like mother-love, risks being seen uncritically as warm, wonderful and quite unproblematic – and indeed, like mother-love, is assumed to be richly rewarding and empowering for both parties' (2000: 141). This statement, contemporaneously, cautions about any oversimplified and glorified notions, while hinting at the complex and challenging landscape of caring relationships.

'Care' and 'caring', as alluded to above, contain ideas about 'caring for' and 'caring about' and raise issues associated with both caring tasks and caring feelings (Parker, 1981; Graham, 1983). Morris (1993) draws attention to the complex nature of 'caring' relationships and highlights that these are not unidimensional but involve reciprocity which is manifested in a variety of ways. Williams (2001) focuses on the 'political ethics of care', and as Featherstone (2004) points out, this is underpinned by 'care' being understood as a complex set of practices which are often rendered natural, invisible or which are marginalized. Williams (2001) and Featherstone (2004) highlight that care of the self and care of others are meaningful activities in their own right and that all of us are involved not simply as givers and receivers, but in a mutual state of interdependence where the social processes of care encompass plurality and diversity. 'Care' also has a gendered component and debates have raged about the tendency, evident in 'community care', to push women into assuming ever greater emotional as well as physical responsibilities (Williams, 1996). As a result, some feminists have placed emphasis on the development, in both the political and policy arenas, of a more rounded concept of citizenship where there is an acknowledgement of the importance of 'care' as an activity and as an orientation. However, again, emphasis is placed on choice, on the importance for women of paid work, on the need to continue to break down gender boundaries and on the complex nature of 'caring' (Williams, 2001; Lister, 2002; Featherstone, 2004).

Clearly, 'care', in all its forms, does not take place in a vacuum. Nor can 'care' be reduced to a formula. 'Care' takes place in the wider socio-economic context and within a cultural framework. In relation to mental health, mental distress and mental ill-health 'care' also has other connotations. As Brechin (2000) points out, care can be regarded as a form of social control. Sayce (2000) recognizes this aspect when she recommends the substitution of the term 'ally' for carer. She states that service users or consumers have to be seen as playing a key role in the articulation of the mental distress they experience and in conveying this experience, together with the forms of support they value, to family members and professionals. She argues that professionals taking on the mantle of the expert and speaking for service users to family members, and family members speaking for service users to professionals, serves to disempower service users, negatively positioning them as being in need of care, and control.

An exploration of family caring brings to the fore tensions between the views of the service user, their recommendations about what works for them, the often differing perspectives of family members and their own support needs. From a philosophical viewpoint, Heidegger posited that people have concerns about the things in their world which he described as *Sorge* to signify 'care' or heedfulness (Polt, 1999). He also described the notion of people 'being with' others as *Fursorge*, which means solicitude. Solicitude was described by Heidegger as providing 'food and clothing, and the nursing of the sick body (Crotty, 1996: 84). Furthermore, in his analysis of solicitude, Heidegger distinguished two forms of 'being with': 'leaping in' which serves to take 'care' away from the person, whereas, 'leaping ahead' acts to give 'care' back to the person. Following this thinking, Benner and Wrubel (1989) argue that 'leaping in' might well be unavoidable in certain sets of circumstances, but it is really 'leaping ahead' which is commended as a form of facilitation and advocacy that helps to empower people. Chang and Horrocks (2006), writing about the lived experiences of Chinese families in Malaysia, suggest that where 'leaping in' care is provided to a family member with a diagnosed mental illness, family 'carers' tend to experience higher degrees of stress. The notion of 'care' brings to the fore tensions between the protection of individuals from risk or harm and the enhancement of autonomy, self-determination and freedom of choice. Within this tension are variations in the degree of responsibility of all parties involved in caring relationships – responsibilities of family members to 'care' without excessive 'leaping-in' tendencies and the responsibility of a family member experiencing distress to demonstrate their 'care' by prioritizing reciprocity.

Family narratives

Narratives from families where a member has experienced mental distress or has been diagnosed with a mental illness give powerful descriptive and impressionistic accounts of 'the lived experience' (Deveson, 1991; Wasow, 1995; Jones, 2002; Greenberg, 2009). These narratives, often recounted with a honesty that is confronting, have contributed towards helping families explore challenges. These narratives also act to position the family as having something to say about mental health, mental distress and illness. Wasow (1995) writes about her own experience of a son with a diagnosed mental illness and her dedication in her research to listening to the 'voices' of other families. What she found was that everyone ended up living in a tower of Babel with the often conflicting and competing voices of a constellation of members in the cast – people experiencing mental distress or with diagnosed mental illnesses, family members, mental health professionals, community groups, advocacy groups, researchers, religious leaders and policy makers. Add to this multiplicity of perspectives, competing theories and issues of aetiology, care and management, and the babel increases.

Wasow (1995) comments: 'As with a large stone skipping across water, the ripple effect of a diagnosis of *mental illness* on the entire family is enormous' (1995: 3). Deveson (1991) found this in her experiences with her adult son, Jonathon, who was diagnosed with schizophrenia. Deveson points to her multiple roles as mother, journalist, broadcaster, writer and film-maker and she says she felt that she became '... Demeter trying to save her child from the underworld' (1991: 3). In her very personal account of the effects of Jonathon's condition on the family, Deveson recognizes that her other two younger children were pushed into 'the shadows' as well as having to grow up fast and '... in that growing, lose much of their childhood' (1991: 3). For Deveson, the lived experience was such that she claims, 'Writing this book has meant re-living periods I would rather forget' (1991: 3) and points out that each member of the family remembers the experience differently, because each of them experienced it in their own way.

In his narrative interviews with families, Jones (2002) highlights the idea of 'family' as an explanatory device. His interviews reveal the commonsense notion of people being bound together by 'family' or 'blood' ties and that their lived experience of stress, uncertainties, challenges and rewards is filtered through these bonds and ties. As his interviews uncover, there is a family commitment, often in relationships which are painful and on the face of it unrewarding. Jones confesses to feeling 'puzzlement' at what keeps family members engaged in seemingly painful relationships from which they appear to gain so little. In particular, Jones expresses his awareness of carrying this attitude of puzzlement into the interviews with siblings, and it is notable that relatively little research has been carried out with siblings. A study by Horwitz et al. (1992) explored the idea that the sibling relationship is a voluntary one rather than an obligatory one in terms of 'care' and family support. Their findings suggest that siblings will often remain involved with a mentally distressed sibling, although a hierarchy of obligation does exist and siblings do not appear to provide support in the same way that parents, spouses and children do.

Scant literature exists concerning the experiences of spouses of people diagnosed with mental health conditions, although spousal desire to receive information about mental illnesses and how to cope was documented as early as 1955 (Deasy and Quinn, 1995). According to unpublished research cited by Wasow (1995), the drop-out rate of spouses from general psycho-educational support groups is high because spousal needs are not usually met in groups where the majority of members are parents of children with diagnosed mental health conditions. In the United States, Wasow reports that this recognition that parents and spouses have different needs and concerns has led to the development of specific spouse support groups. Spouses complain about frequently feeling they are not understood – by extended family members, friends, family doctors, psychiatrists and clergy. They also draw attention to feeling neglected with other family members and friends dropping away, and even if such relationships are maintained the unpredictability of their lives results in feelings of social isolation (Bernheim et al., 1982). Carol Grogan, an advocate of spouse support groups, laments, 'You couldn't conceive of a situation in which a relative wouldn't call you if your wife had severe diabetes. But if it's mental illness, forget it. No calls, no casseroles, nothing' (cited in Wasow, 1995: 61). Many spouses have raised concerns about feeling excluded by professionals, and they make it clear that they want to be responded to as equal partners (Pejiert, 2001). On a positive note, Grogan notes that in the spouse support groups, 'We all find relief... lots of laughter. We share clippings, books, suggestions and "doctor" stories. Our time together is precious, funny and sad' (cited in Wasow, 1995: 64).

As far back as 1983, Troll commented on the role of grandparents in the US families. Children were said to view their grandparents as the most significant people in their lives, after their parents. Yet, little information on the role of grandparents in a family affected by mental distress or illness has been recorded (Marsh, 1992; Wasow, 1995). No support groups exist for grandparents, and many of those interviewed by Wasow said they wanted more information about mental health and mental illness and how to be more supportive. Some reported feeling guilty that their age and infirmity prevented them from taking a more active role.

Overall, the voices of personal experience have been powerfully presented in the narrative accounts of people in various family situations – parents, children, spouses and siblings. Such accounts highlight the complexity of confused feelings generated as well as the varying perspectives presented by many different voices. Living in a tower of Babel has its advantages – differing points of view get a hearing, and although it is difficult to draw conclusions, the diversity as well as the commonality of experiences are brought to the fore.

Families and 'care'

Over the past few decades, there has been a significant quantity of research conducted about various aspects of mental distress/illness experienced by family members. In 1990, Maurin and Boyd cautioned regarding the difficulty in interpreting the findings '... because of various methodological problems or inconsistencies among studies' (1990: 100). Since that time, many more studies have been undertaken, some focusing on individual stories and some paying particular attention to socio-cultural aspects, yet the caution issued by Maurin and Boyd remains. Interpretation of research findings is fraught with challenges regarding not only methodological concerns but also issues related to the appropriateness of generalizability. Most research continues to be pursued from a Western perspective, and as highlighted earlier, this presupposes either a scientific or alternatively postmodernist world and worldview, which raises further issues about the applicability to other cultures and contexts.

As highlighted, the provision of support and 'care' within families is complex (Rose, 1998; Gray et al., 2009) and different and complimentary roles in different constellations are taken on at different times (Keith, 1995, Gray et al., 2009). What has emerged from both narrative accounts and research studies are both the strengths and the challenges of family support or family 'care'.

Looking at the advent of family support and 'care' from a historical perspective, it is notable that from the 1960s until the early 1980s, ideas about the treatment of schizophrenia were influenced by theoretical perspectives which 'blamed' the 'schizophrenic' influence of the family. As Bland et al. (2009) point out, studies carried out by Vaughn and Leff (1976) and Hooley (1985) focused on the contribution of various family traits, such as hostility, emotional over-involvement and an overly critical stance in the production of toxic emotional environments which could promote the development or relapse of conditions such as schizophrenia and bipolar disorder. Later, attention turned to the family's role as 'caregivers' and to the 'burden' of 'care' (Lefley, 1987b; Hatfield, 1997). Here, emphasis was placed on the crises caused in families by the diagnosis of a mental illness with attention being drawn particularly to experiences of stigma, isolation and the taking on of heavy responsibilities (Platt, 1985; Lefley, 1987a; Wasow, 1995; Hatfield, 1997; Gilbert, 1998).

Since the advent of deinstitutionalization, many family members have found themselves being positioned as 'informal carers' (Leggatt, 2007). As Bytheway and Johnson (1998) point out, the term 'carer 'is a relatively recent construction, and they emphasize that family members in the 1950s' operating as 'carers' would not have used this word, nor would they have thought of themselves as belonging to a particular category of people. Governments, particularly in Western nations, have relatively recently woken up to the ways in which family 'carers', operating in a range of arenas, save exchequers enormous sums of money, and increasingly policy documents have recognized both the significance as well as the support needs of 'carers'. In 2002, in Australia, Standard 2 of the National Standards for the Mental Health Workforce stated that:

> Mental health professionals encourage and support the participation of consumers and 'carers' in determining (or influencing) their individual treatment and care. They also actively promote, encourage and support the participation of consumers, family members and/or 'carers' in the planning, implementation and evaluation of mental health service delivery'.

(National Standards for the Mental Health Workforce, 2002: 11)

As we have seen in Chapter 3, in England and Wales, the 1998 National Carers' Strategy underlined the government's commitment to improving information and support for 'carers', and in 1999 the National Service Framework for Mental Health included a standard relating to the needs of carers. Standard Six 'Caring about carers' specifically articulates the aim of providing care to meet carers needs and recognizes that they play a vital role in the mental health system (1999: 69). In 2003, the then British Prime Minister, Tony Blair, acknowledged the role and responsibilities of carers generally, saying he was not '... speaking of abstract ideas, but of real people and real events; the things many people do to make things better for those around them' (as quoted in Lester and Glasby, 2006: 204). Tony Blair went on to sing carers praises by calling their work 'extraordinary' and ending with the statement, 'Carers are among the unsung heroes of British life' (as quoted in Lester and Glasby, 2006: 205). By publicly emphasizing the determination and dedication of 'carers', Tony Blair effectively embedded the role of 'carers' into policy and practice.

However, despite such rhetoric, many 'carers' do not want to 'care' and feel forced into roles they do not want because of a lack of services. Support for 'carers', although increasing, also incorporates a strong aspirational component (Fawcett and Karban, 2005; Bland et al., 2009). A further major criticism of current policy with regard to 'carers' is an implicit assumption that they comprise a single category of people with similar needs, rather than individuals and families with diverse and different perspectives, wants and aspirations (Arskey et al., 2002). Arskey et al. (2002) caution against adopting an over-simplistic view that risks neglecting the needs of individual caregivers, and in particular those 'carers' who belong to marginalized groups, for instance, black and minority ethnic 'carers', 'carers' supporting more than one person and less recognized caring situations, for example, 'caring' in gay and lesbian relationships, or 'caring' at a distance. They also suggest that support services should be underpinned by four key principles. These are that they should be 'positive and inclusive', 'flexible and individualized', 'accessible and responsive' and 'integrated and co-ordinated' (Arskey et al., 2002).

Another group of carers – young people caring for a parent experiencing mental distress or with a diagnosed mental illness – have only relatively recently started to receive attention.

According to Aldridge and Becker (2003), where professionals engage with 'young carers' in a respectful and helpful manner by acknowledging their needs and by providing forms of support valued as appropriate, 'young carers' are provided with some degree of choice regarding informal 'caring' arrangements. Often professional help is highly valued by the family, although there is evidence which points to professionals failing to engage in effective intervention strategies and offering service-directed forms of assistance rather than person-focused support (Aldridge and Becker, 2003).

Not all children of parents who experience mental distress/illness will have the ability or resources to provide support or to become 'carers'. For many children, even as adult children, the message to the world might well be more a 'help me' one as they experience helplessness and isolation. Gloria Steinem, writing about her experience as a young person with a mother with a diagnosed mental illness, says, 'But my ultimate protection was this: I was just passing through; a guest in the house; perhaps this wasn't my mother at all' (1983: 49). Research focusing on young people coping with a troubled parent highlights the enormous variation in coping strategies and differentiates between young people who desperately need support and those who appear to manage (Gorell Barnes, 1996; Marlowe, 1996). Such young people may live their daily lives with interrupted routines, expectations that they keep the household running and loss of positive parental input into their development. Factors that buffer children from the everyday reality of the stressful experience of mental distress/illness can include the presence of a second, supportive parent in the home; supportive outside relationships with other adults; and membership of sporting or religious groups – with all of these involving relationships and interactions where the young person's positive self-concept can be nurtured (Gorell Barnes, 1996).

In Britain, a recent report published by the BBC suggests that there are four times more 'young carers' in the United Kingdom than are officially recognized and that an application of these survey results to the United Kingdom as a whole would result in a total of around 700,000 young people providing forms of assistance to their parents or relatives (BBC, 2010). For the past 20 years, 'young carers' have been identified as needing specialist services (Bilsborrow, 1992; Marlowe, 1996; Aldridge and Becker,

2003), and self-help groups (such as the Network), together with academic bodies (such as the Young Carers Research Group at Loughborough University), have played an active role in awareness raising for 'young carers' in the general community. As with 'care' generally, caring by young people takes place in situations characterized by reciprocity and shared 'care'. However, when looking at 'care' in terms of personal assistance, 'young carers' have foregrounded the importance of a range of easily accessible and non-threatening support options and have particularly emphasized the utility of the internet and independent advocacy services (Aldridge and Becker, 2003: Fawcett et al., 2004).

Individuals and families

As seen elsewhere in this book (particularly in Chapters 1 and 2), Bracken and Thomas (2005) in relation to postpsychiatry emphasize the importance of new possibilities emerging in mental health. They acknowledge the challenges posed by the needs of pharmaceutical companies and the expedient policies of governments which serve to push psychiatry down a very narrow path. However, despite these constraints, they foreground the importance of ending the 'monologue of reason about madness' (Bracken and Thomas, 2005: 20). They do not want to formulate new models, which they view as part of the current problem, nor return to past critiques, rather they want to increase diversity and draw attention to complexity and contradictions, to highlight that framing distress as a technical problem can have serious negative problems for individuals, families and communities, and to face up to science's ability to obscure and silence as well as to illuminate and liberate. These new possibilities clearly have the potential to reconfigure relationships in a range of directions and to open up different pathways through the labyrinth of current understandings of mental health, mental distress and illness.

Consumer movements in mental health, as previously highlighted, draw from critical and social approaches to mental health and illness, to highlight power imbalances, the experiences, hopes and aspirations of consumers, the iatrogenic effects of neuroleptic medication and the importance of hope and of consumer-defined notions of recovery (Bracken and Thomas, 2005; Fawcett and Karban, 2005; Macfarlane, 2009). As Spandler and Carlton (2009) point out (and this is also highlighted in

Chapter 6), 'recovery' as interpreted by consumers and service users is often contrasted with medicalized notions of the treatment–cure continuum, and it is used as a means of challenging the traditional priorities of mental health services. It focuses on a person achieving a satisfying, hopeful and contributing life, irrespective of a mental health diagnosis. It is notable that these movements have generally taken issue with the notion of 'care' defined as something which they, as service users or consumers, are in need of, which constitutes a burden for others and which implies that others need to manage their daily lives. Sayce (2000), writing of her relationship with a partner diagnosed with manic depression, comments that what they have is ' ... a mutual relationship, not one in which "care" goes one way, and not one involving "burden" (an offensive term that should be dropped)' (2000: 11). As highlighted at the beginning of this chapter, it is important to widen the discussion from what might be considered a useful shorthand term – 'carer' – to consider all the implications of 'caring'. This broader discussion clearly needs to take place in the context of daily life, where full account is taken of complex social factors and where consideration is also given to a health care system which is often stretched for funding and resources and where prevailing custom and practice takes precedence over appraisal and innovation.

Concluding remarks

'Care' does not take place in a vacuum. Nor can 'care' be reduced to a formula. Care takes place in the wider socio-economic context and within a cultural framework. Consequently, 'caring relationships' are always open, subject to change and are never straightforward. In this chapter, we have drawn attention to the complexities of 'care', 'caring' and family relationships and to the different perspectives that have proved influential at different points in time. The notion of 'care' in the arena of mental health and mental distress and illness contains many elements. Some of these are constructive and positive, others negative and unhelpful. Families under stress and experiencing distress do require external support. The form that this takes clearly has to be flexible, well resourced and collaborative. Responses need to be sensitive, adaptable, tailored to particular situations and inclusive. Overall, we argue that the notion of 'care' cannot be narrowly prescribed and that it always carries with it a plethora of meanings, interpretations and operational identities. Clearly, 'caring' conversations will continue for some time to come.

In our next chapter, we locate the discussion with the broad framework of social inclusion policies and focus specifically on the challenges faced by those who work in the mental health arena. As part of this process, we consider the utility of practices which draw from anti-discriminatory and anti-oppressive principles, critical reflection, and from spatial analysis and action.

CHAPTER 10

Anti-Discriminatory Practice in Mental Health

Throughout this book, mental well-being and mental ill-health have been viewed as dynamic and constructive and as open to a range of understandings and meanings which reflect context, the constantly changing interaction between an individual and their environment and the ways in which these are interpreted. As part of this process, the influence of a range of perspectives, with some clearly being much more dominant and informing what we take for granted than others, has been reviewed. In this chapter, we particularly consider the role of professionals and appraise the significance of operating principles associated with anti-discriminatory and anti-oppressive practice and critical reflection. We also review the concept of social inclusion and the opportunities and constraints that this social policy platform has brought to the arena of mental health and well-being. In the light of this discussion, we consider a form of spatial analysis linked to social entrepreneurship which, given its basis in anti-oppressive and anti-discriminatory practice and critical reflection, has the capacity to inform community-orientated responses to mental health.

Setting the scene

Consumer movements, which have placed emphasis on social understandings of mental health, have challenged discriminatory attitudes and stigma. They have directed attention towards the importance of acknowledging difference and diversity and have countered claims of dangerous 'loonies' with statistics which, as we have seen in Chapter 3, show that only a very small number of violent acts are carried out by those who are known to be experiencing mental health problems (Taylor and Gunn, 1999; Mindframe, 2010). Also, as highlighted in Chapter 7, concepts of 'risk' and 'vulnerability' can be reframed and rather than referring to a specific and static grouping can apply to all of us in a variety of guises at various points in our lives.

Thompson and Thompson (2008) pertinently state that when good ideas become popular there is an accompanying danger that they will become oversimplified and used in a superficial way. An inevitable consequence is that they will also fail to do justice to the complexities involved. Thompson and Thompson (2008) specifically critique the notion that theories and knowledge generally can be applied directly to practice in a prescribed manner. Drawing from Schön, they regard such an approach as falling under the auspices of 'technical rationality' which Schön regarded as a 'positivist epistemology of practice' (Schön, 1983: 31 in Thompson and Thompson, 2008: 14). They maintain that the adoption of such an approach reduces human service professionals to technicians where their role becomes limited and they are required to implement set procedures in a standardized manner rather than to innovate and direct. Many would argue that human service professionals have been subject to such reductionist working practices as part of the implementation of New Public Management policies and practices in the 1990s. Healy (2009) draws attention to the increasing dominance of a technocratic approach across a wide range of major policy and planning arenas in Australia and to the shortfalls that this produces. Authors in this field challenge mental health professionals to become proactive rather than reactive and to use anti-oppressive and anti-discriminatory practice and critical reflection to address disadvantage, stigma, discrimination and social exclusion (Sayce, 2000; Wilson and Beresford, 2002; Thompson and Thompson, 2008; Fook, 2009). These working practices will now be appraised in greater detail.

Anti-oppressive and anti-discriminatory practice

Anti-oppressive and anti-discriminatory practice has been influenced by a variety of intertwined theoretical perspectives which have included structurally orientated social analyses, the critical edge of the various feminisms as well as arguments drawn from critical theory. These have variously served to illustrate pervasive class and social inequalities as well as institutional and individual discrimination associated with the intersecting dimensions of gender, 'race', sexuality and disability. It is notable that in the 1980s and 1990s, these influences often acquired a well-intentioned but prescriptive edge. In the United Kingdom in particular, these tendencies led to what many described as the introduction of an oppressive degree of political correctness into professional training in anti-oppressive and anti-discriminatory practice (Thompson, 2006). Ironically, in many respects, anti-oppressive and anti-discriminatory practice at this particular historical juncture can be seen to have fallen victim to the application of 'technical rationalities'.

However, anti-oppressive and anti-discriminatory practice has continued to be re-forged and re-developed with universal principles increasingly taking account of the nuances of context. The operation of power imbalances has also been foregrounded and clear links have been made between anti-oppressive and anti-discriminatory practice and the maintenance of ethical standards. Here, ethical professional awareness has to be accompanied by a concomitant focus on addressing discrimination, as well as authoritarianism and inconsistency. These challenges have ensured that anti-oppressive and anti-discriminatory practices in the second decade of the twenty-first century continue to maintain a critical edge and the emphasis placed on the operation of power imbalances, on inequity and on the ways in which diversity and difference can so easily slide into division has ensured that anti-oppressive and anti-discriminatory practice retains significant relevance.

As we have highlighted throughout this book, terminology is important and as such it is pertinent to explore the meanings that can be ascribed to 'diversity' and 'division' at this point, particularly given the relevance of these terms for a discussion of anti-oppressive and anti-discriminatory practice. As Williams (1996) emphasizes, 'diversity' can be viewed as a positive and constructive concept, and we can all be seen to hold a diverse range of attitudes and opinions as well as belong to a range of social networks which in turn reflect family and individual interests. As a consequence a diverse society can be valued and regarded as rich and as socially enhancing. However, a diverse society can also be regarded by some as a problem. There may be a dominant group, culture or political system which is suspicious of, threatened by or simply dismissive of anything that appears to be 'not the same as' or which deviates from what is viewed as appropriate, customary or normal. This is when diversity can transmogrify into division and when those who are perceived to be 'different' or who do not appear to conform to prevailing social conventions lose value, are viewed negatively and become subject to prejudice and negative discrimination.

The recognition of negative discrimination can have positive results and can lead to affirmative action. This is where negative valuations and stigma are recognized and attempts are made through policy and practice to effect redress. However, negative discrimination can be pervasive and can result in the unfavourable treatment of all those assigned to a particular category as a result of socially or individually prescribed combinations of ethnicity, gender, sexuality or disability. As discussed throughout this book, mental ill-health features strongly in relation to such negative prescriptions and although a variety of campaigns often portraying very different messages (ranging from mental ill-health being viewed an illness like any other which can affect anyone of us, to a celebration by consumer groups of 'mad pride') have had an effect, negative discrimination remains strong and pervasive.

Two perspectives of power

As highlighted earlier, a discussion of negative forms of discrimination leads inevitably to a focus on power, as its constituents relate specifically to power imbalances operating in a variety of ways at individual, institutional and social levels. However, it does need to be acknowledged that 'power' can be conceptualized in a number of different ways and it is useful to look at two in more detail as these form useful points of contrast. The first, drawing from Sawicki (1991), can be called a 'juridical–hierarchical' perspective. This can be seen to represent the most commonly held view of how power operates, and it is regarded as being underpinned by national and international laws and policies. Within this formulation, power tends to be referred to as being specifically located in a particular area, or with a particular group, or as a possession which some have and others do not. Accordingly, power is regarded as the particular preserve of the most powerful groups and institutions in any society. It is also seen to operate in a hierarchical manner and to be imposed. An example relates to white westernized men being generally seen to have more power than white westernized women or non-white westernized men, and the hierarchical ordering continues with those 'with' mental health problems having far less power than those 'without'.

Overall then, within this conceptualization of power (and it is recognized that this discussion is a pared down account of this perspective), power tends to be regarded as an entity which some have and others do not. As a result, it is applied in a 'top-down' manner and operates repressively in that it can be seen to be predominately about those with power determining what those without should do, with sanctions and penalties being applied for non-compliance (Fawcett, 2000a).

A contrasting view is a social relational view of power. This draws from the work of Michel Foucault (1973, 1977, 1980a, b, 1981), and key points of difference with a juridical-hierarchical perspective are that power is not viewed as a thing which some possess and others do not, rather it is conceptualized as more of a process. Importantly, as part of this process, power is not regarded as being imposed, but as always circulating by means of social interaction and everyday social practices. As a result, rather than power being used to divide those who, by virtue of position, are seen to posses power from those who do not, we are all regarded as using power in a variety of ways as part of our daily activities and by means of how we relate to one another. As a result, power is seen to operate from the 'bottom-up' rather than from the 'top-down'. However, within this conceptualization, although we are all seen to use and abuse power, particular power frameworks still operate fuelled by the operation of 'taken-for-granted' world views. These, in turn form what, from a critical deconstructive viewpoint, can be regarded as dominant discourses. An example of the operation of a dominant discourse from this particular perspective would be the current emphasis placed on medicalized or clinical understandings of mental health being the only way of understanding or responding to a lack of mental well-being. Accordingly, attention is drawn towards the implications of the power and knowledge frameworks of mental health 'experts' being afforded a greater value within daily interaction than the experiential knowledge and power of consumers or service users. This perspective of power facilitates a deconstructive appraisal and draws attention to how power can be seen to be both circulating and used by all of us to support, but also to challenge, prevailing views.

Taking on board these understandings of power and looking again at anti-oppressive and anti-discriminatory practice, it can be asserted that viewing power as a thing which some have and some do not, or which can be conferred by one group upon another, is often unhelpful. Regarding power and empowering practices as processes, however, can be constructive as this draws attention to the ways in which power circulates and is employed by all of us to varying degrees to support or to challenge particular positions or discourses. Deconstructive appraisal in turn serves to draw attention to how dominant positions or discourses can include some groups and exclude others and how some understandings or perspectives can be mainstreamed, and become accepted and taken for granted, and others marginalized.

Overall, anti-oppressive and anti-discriminatory practice challenges complacency and taken-for-granted assumptions. It also militates against the adoption of reductionist models in that it is not about applying a straightforward formula, but rather focuses on what is going on, what effect this is having and on whom. It is also about exploring ways of both drawing attention to and addressing these areas. This gives practice a political edge, in that it places mental health professionals in a prime position to work with others, to identify inequity and discrimination, to agree aims and objectives and to put in place strategies for change.

Critical reflection

Critical reflection incorporates many of the deconstructive elements associated with the underpinning principles of anti-discriminatory and anti-oppressive practice. Although the concept of critical reflection draws from many disciplines and professions, it can broadly be seen to be about being self-aware, about critically and constructively reviewing and learning from all situations and about taking account of contextually specific factors. Critical reflection incorporates making links between experience and knowledge and accepting that relationships between knowledge and power need to be subject to ongoing critical investigation. As a result, experience is regarded as being constantly in flux and subject to ongoing processes of interpretation and evaluation. Fook (2009), for example, maintains that critical reflection 'involves learning from experience by examining fundamental assumptions, reintegrating experiences and as part of this process, reformulating meaning and principles for living which lead to new guidelines for action' (Fook, AASSWE Presentation, 2009). Within this, she makes it clear that experience is made up of many different aspects which include emotion, thoughts, action and interpretation, intersected by cultural, structural and gendered considerations. Many authors (and these include Fook, 2002, 2009; Thompson and Thompson, 2008) have developed questions for promoting critical reflection and these can be reformulated to include the following:

- Reviewing how we view knowledge
- Looking at why some forms of knowledge are valued over other forms at particular points in time
- Critically exploring how we have acquired knowledge and what has informed this process
- Focusing on our own values and those of our professions and questioning their universal and particular relevance
- Taking account of our emotions and those of others
- Actively learning from experience and creating dynamic practice experience
- Looking at context and making intercontextual connections
- In any situation, planning a strategy which incorporates the basic tenets of:
  - What is currently happening?
  - What are the different assumptions operating?
  - What are the strengths as well as the problems associated with these different assumptions?
  - What do we (used inclusively to refer to all those involved) want to do or not do?
  - How are we going to operationalize this?
  - How are we going to evaluate the outcomes?
  - How do we learn from this process?
  - What might we have done differently?
  - How might we transfer this learning to other contexts?

These considerations and questions not only focus on unpacking the various assumptions and value judgements operating in any situation but also take account of the power dynamics involved.

They also make links with theoretical perspectives and emphasize the utility of a participative approach to decision-making. This assists in the production of action strategies and in the formulation of a means of continually reflecting on both processes as well as outcomes.

An example of the operation of this way of working could relate to a human service professional being contacted by a local councillor as a result of an eight-year-old boy being caught spray painting the wall of a local garage. The councillor reports that the boy's mother is thought to be mentally ill, and his teachers think that he might be suffering from attention deficit hyperactivity disorder. The adoption of a critically reflective approach would initially focus on exploring the range of assumptions that appear to be operating. These could include the situation being viewed as a 'one off' example of high spirits, as a serious case of antisocial behaviour, as an indication that the boy's mother cannot cope, as a sign that the boy is being subject to undue pressure as a result of his mother's assumed condition or as an illustration that he has a mental health problem. The process of critical reflection directs an exploratory lens towards the posing of analytical questions relating to where these assumptions have come from, how these are being substantiated and, with regard to all the different views operating, which or whose is being privileged. Using critical reflection in this way involves critically appraising all of these scenarios, fully involving the boy and his mother, together with the other players, in a review of the situation, negotiating a constructive responsive strategy and continually reviewing and reflecting on the process as well as the outcomes.

It is clear from this example that critical reflection is not a simplistic or prescriptive undertaking. It is also a way of working that promotes partnership and the active participation of all involved. This does not mean that experiences are taken at face value, but that they are used as the starting point for an inclusive journey, which by the continual posing of critical questions can deepen and extend the range of the reflective analysis and the resulting action.

Addressing social exclusion

Anti-oppressive and anti-discriminatory practice and critical reflection have a core focus on addressing social exclusion and fostering social inclusion. The concept of social inclusion has featured significantly in social policy in both the United Kingdom and Australia in recent times and can be seen as a way of reconfiguring more structurally orientated discussions associated with inequality, social division and citizenship. Clearly, stigma, negative discrimination and marginalization all contribute to social exclusion and those diagnosed as having mental health problems, as has been highlighted throughout this book, walk a slippery path within medicalizing discourses being variously regarded as ill (with mental illness being equated to physical conditions as a means of reducing stigma), as being the subject of ongoing risk assessments (with regard to the dangers they might pose both to themselves and others, particularly if they cease taking prescribed medication) and as patients (with individual pathology and prognosis being largely prioritized over social and environmental factors). The concept of social inclusion facilitates the making of wider connections linked to social structures and embedded inequalities. A brief review of the origins of social inclusion and social exclusion can prove helpful in assessing the contribution that these concepts make to practice within the mental health arena overall.

Social inclusion, as a political and social concept, can be seen to have emanated from the establishment of an interdisciplinary Social Exclusion Unit by the newly elected Blair government in the United Kingdom in 1997. This was quickly followed by the creation of similar bodies in Scotland and Northern Ireland and by the formulation of a range of policy initiatives and a wide-ranging social inclusion agenda. Underpinning these developments was the identification of social exclusion as a divisive social issue and one which militated against the Labour government's creation of a social investment state with its concomitant focus on utilizing and expanding the productivity and capacity of all citizens and communities. In England and Wales, Scotland and Northern Ireland, three main aspects were emphasized. These related to 'New Deals' for disabled people, including those with mental health problems, lone parents and those experiencing unemployment; the regeneration of poor neighbourhoods through new funding programmes; and the adoption of a 'joined up' approach by government departments to improve access to services as well as providing more user friendly responses. In 2009, the Social Exclusion Unit was disbanded and replaced by a Communities and Local Government structure, responsible to government ministers, but governed by a board made up of local and central government members and officials and supported by quasi-government organizations, with a presence in the Cabinet Office (Fawcett et al., 2010). The brief was to continue to address social exclusion and foster social inclusion but to concentrate on further embedding existing policies rather than to develop new initiatives. The 2010 general election in the United Kingdom resulted in a further change of direction and the wide-ranging cuts to the public sector have served to sideline both social inclusion and social exclusion agendas.

In Australia, 'A Stronger, Fairer Australia (Commonwealth of Australia, 2009) has focused on promoting social inclusion rather than identifying social exclusion. The strategic direction of the social inclusion agenda has served to emphasize the different political emphasis adopted by the Rudd and Gillard governments, over the 'user pays' individualized and market-orientated policies of the previous Howard-led Liberal/National Coalition. However, the underlying principles and the emphasis placed on a social investment state remain very similar to the general direction pioneered by all four countries within the United Kingdom.

In Australia, as well as in the United Kingdom overall, although social exclusion/inclusion has placed emphasis on the ways in which disadvantage is both connected and multi-dimensional, the importance of economic participation has remained a major focal point. As a result, the undertaking of paid work has served to dominate debates relating to rights, responsibilities and the benefits of citizenship. The employment of adults deemed capable of work has been a major platform of benefit reform and in Australia, as well as in the United Kingdom generally, levels of benefit have been adjusted in accordance with an individual's assessed capability for work. As a result, those deemed able to work, at least in a part-time capacity, have been placed on different and often reduced allowances and have been required to actively seek paid employment. In 2008, the Rudd-led Federal government in Australia brought in measures to further reduce disincentives to seeking work. These included the provision that those people in receipt of the Disability Support Pension who used employment services to find work were no longer subject to an automatic review of their eligibility for the

Disability Support Pension. The National Mental Health and Disability Employment Strategy, unveiled by the Rudd government in Australia in 2009, also made more money available to both promote work opportunities and provide additional support to those seeking work. In England and Wales similarly, there has been a strong emphasis on 'work first' policies.

Major criticisms of such policies, particularly in the arena of mental health, relate to 'work first' benefit requirements not being adequately supplemented by the availability of support services to provide assistance to those in work as well as to those adversely affected by workplace casualization policies. As a result, critics maintain that the accompanying need to continually have to reclaim benefits, with the stress and hardship that this entails, has been insufficiently addressed. The effect of work-orientated compliance strategies on those for whom paid work may not be a passport to social inclusion has also been emphasized by many (Bellamy and Cowling, 2008; Fawcett, 2009).

Nevertheless, despite such critiques, a review of the prioritized areas contained in social inclusion strategies makes it clear that the view that paid employment leads to greater inclusion and equality remains strong amongst government bodies. The Australian Social Inclusion Board's (2010) synopsis of what social inclusion means further exemplifies this continued policy emphasis. This synopsis prioritizes four key elements. These relate to

(1) learning, and the importance of all young people participating in education and training;
(2) working, with all assessed as being eligible, participating in employment or in unpaid or voluntary work which includes family and carer responsibilities;
(3) engaging and connecting with local communities, by using local services and participating in cultural, civic and recreational activities; and
(4) having a voice, by engaging with community programmes.

It is notable that in relation to the associated monitoring and reporting framework for these four key areas, which look at both headline and supplementary indicators, employment rates are seen to be better measures of social inclusion than unemployment or participation rates. Clearly, this emphasis not only serves to further reinforce the primary status ascribed to employment, but also relegates other aspects to subsidiary and dependent positions. Within the context of this overall discussion, it is pertinent to note that the attention paid to employment, to productivity and to maximizing capacity rather than to managing dependency in the arena of mental health has, rather paradoxically, further reinforced, rather than reduced, the focus on compliance. This is because compliance with medication can easily become a prerequisite for compliance with becoming a job seeker, which in turn can so easily become a requirement for the conferring of the rights of citizenship. Fawcett et al. (2010) maintain, in the context of an analysis of welfare to work policies, that a 'work first' approach to 'activating' excluded members of the community is likely to have as many costs as benefits with competing requirements, pressures and funding issues coming to the fore. They maintain that addressing social exclusion by prioritizing paid work fails to systemically address those pervasive inequalities associated with low income, the casualization of the workplace, poor educational opportunities and unequal access to health services. As a result, addressing marginalization and exclusion and the accompanying negative constructions can be seen to require the adoption of a much broader perspective that not only uses the existing policy space opened up by the social inclusion agenda but also significantly expands upon it. In this, mental health professionals can be seen to have an important role to play.

Mental health professionals: spatial analysis and social entrepreneurship

The preceding discussion makes it clear that professionals working in the arena of mental health need to engage constructively with the various manifestations of the social inclusion agenda by drawing from anti-oppressive and anti-discriminatory principles and practice and by utilizing an ongoing process of critical reflection. Fawcett and Hanlon (2009a) point to the importance of practitioners, particularly those operating in community settings, identifying and using those policy spaces opened up by the current emphasis on social inclusion to re-forge social connections at a range of levels and to re-energize community involvement and participation. They argue that an emphasis on flexible tools such as spatial analysis and social entrepreneurship can enable practitioners to effectively build capacity and to foster inclusive process and practices. At this point, it is worth looking at such flexible tools in a little more detail.

Spatial analysis (and this discussion also draws from the work of Duncan, 1998) focuses on critically examining what is going on in any situation. As with anti-oppressive and anti-discriminatory practice and critical reflection (and indeed spatial analysis and social entrepreneurship form a related configuration), this analysis explores and critically interrogates power imbalances. It looks at the effects of these on the various players and, with a critically reflective lens, identifies strengths as well as discriminatory aspects. The social entrepreneurship element then explores how to facilitate participation, how to ensure that all players are involved in decision-making processes and how a negotiatory framework can be utilized to mediate at a range of levels. In giving an example of how this form of analysis and action can operate, cautionary attention needs to be directed towards the ways in which flexible tools can be translated into rigid applications which have the opposite effect to the one intended.

When applying spatial analysis and social entrepreneurship to any area, at the outset it is important to identify what is going on and the range of expectations and understandings operating. This involves exploring the differences between and within different groups, as well as finding areas where there might be common ground. There might be conflict, for example, about the establishment of a 'Hearing Voices' network in a particular region. Conflict may be associated with competing discourses relating to the professional management of 'risk', to the importance ascribed to those diagnosed with a mental illness continuing to take prescribed medication, to those wanting to focus on stories of courage, optimism, determination and hope, to those wanting to explore alternative or additional ways of managing their voices. Spatial analysis facilitates the teasing out of the key issues and the significance that these have for the different players. A social entrepreneurship approach then uses this analysis to promote creative mediation and to formulate inclusive action strategies. In the example given, there would need to be an acknowledgment of the prevailing issues, with each interest group identifying opportunities, constraints and aspirations. Attention would also need to be paid to the powerplays and power imbalances operating at the different levels, to identifying where there are strategic spaces and to maximising the opportunities available – so one form of action could be to use champions to publicize the strengths of hearing voices networks. This could include bringing in someone who is valued from outside, such as a respected community figure, as a means of re-negotiating engagement or spearheading a form of interactive media involvement.

Throughout it is about identifying areas for negotiation, looking at where tradeoffs can take place and, where there have been small successes, on looking at how these can be built on, sustained and further developed. It is about being creative, innovative and pragmatic and either creating situations or using situations which present themselves to take forward what has been learned and to transform analysis into action. So another example would be to forge a consensus around a single issue which could be a festival about mental health and well-being, which could then at different points be linked to other initiatives such as a community mental health forum, a 'fun' run, consumer/mental health professional lunches and so on. These activities would incorporate the setting up of representative opportunities across different groups at different levels to address barriers and to ensure that agreed action has a clear focus and achievable goals. As highlighted earlier, an ongoing priority is to ensure that the spaces identified by the analysis are strategically utilized and these could also include those found in local councils, service provider agencies more generally, local media outlets, educational establishments, central government schemes and so on. The focus overall is on foregrounding inclusive involvement in decision-making processes at a range of levels, making sure that decisions made are clearly followed through and supported, and that regular feedback is generated.

Spatial analysis linked to social entrepreneurship form a pragmatic way of operating that is integrally associated with anti-oppressive and anti-discriminatory practice and critical reflection. This approach serves as a means of connecting analysis to action recognising that in the arena of mental health any action requires analysis and any analysis requires action. Mental health professionals at all levels are in the firing line and they can feel overwhelmed by pressures to produce tangible outcomes linked to particular rationales or to targeted practices. Nevertheless, the importance of, to use a cliché, continually looking outside the box, of fully taking account of a range of perspectives and of promoting participation and involving individuals and groups in processes which affect them, cannot be underestimated.

Concluding remarks

In this chapter, we have looked at the role of mental health professionals and have explored the utility of ways of working that incorporate anti-oppressive and anti-discriminatory principles as well as processes of critical reflection. We have also appraised how the current emphasis on social inclusion can be used to further open up policy and practice spaces for analysis and action. In all of this, we have not underestimated the difficulties faced by mental health professionals operating in situations beset by scarce resources and prescriptive policies. Rather, what we have sought to do is to emphasize opportunities and to explore ways in which mental health professionals and consumers/service users can work together to bring about change.

Concluding Remarks

In this book, we have paid considerable attention to historical, social and ideological contexts and to the importance of intertwined power and knowledge frameworks. As part of this process, we have highlighted the ongoing influence of modernist ways of thinking in the mental health arena. The prevailing concern with managing 'risk', determining capacity and prescribing particular forms of practice can be clearly associated with a continuing modernist preoccupation with the establishment of certainty. Modernist ways of thinking can also be identified in the still-prevalent tenet that although social, cultural and environmental factors should be taken into account, it still remains possible to identify and separate mental illness or mental disorder from these aspects as well as from the experiential knowledge of those experiencing mental distress. It is also notable that a search for certainty can all too easily serve to blur the identification of the beneficiary. Accordingly, it can become increasingly unclear as to whether 'risk' refers to risk to the public from an individual experiencing mental distress, is associated with protecting an individual perceived as vulnerable from possible harm (with this increasingly being defined solely in physical rather than in holistic and emotional terms) or is employed as a means of protecting professionals or agencies from the repercussions of a particular decision. In this book, we have drawn attention to the pitfalls of a quest for certainty and have argued that uncertainty is a viable option as are a range of understandings of mental well-being and distress which at times take issue with, and at other times complement, dominant views.

In developing the themes and arguments within this book, we have focused on mental health issues across the lifespan and have critically but constructively appraised matters relating to children, young people, adults and older people, acknowledging throughout the diversity of these groupings. We have also looked at vistas and landscapes associated with 'dual diagnoses', families and 'caring', and have explored considerations for mental health practitioners working across a range of settings, from the public to the private and from the clinical to community. In relation to practitioners, the key aspects we have focused on have included anti-oppressive and anti-discriminatory practice, critical reflection as well as spatial analysis and social entrepreneurship. Throughout all of the associated discussions, we have drawn attention to those experiencing mental distress across the lifespan, wanting their stories, their understandings, their hopes and aspirations, and their uniqueness to be fully taken on board and for responses to be inclusive and relevant.

What we have sought to do within this book is to promote critical but constructive analysis and to highlight the contribution that can be made by innovative, flexible, creative and adaptable practices. Above all, we have emphasized that we all experience mental distress in varying degrees throughout our life span and we are all involved in varying capacities and to varying extents in this dynamic arena. The challenge for each of us is to work together to develop a range of understandings and responses that reflect our differences as well as providing us with forms of support that enhance rather than diminish our lives.

References

Abrams, R. (1989) Out of the Blue: The Rehabilitation of Electroconvulsive Therapy. *The Sciences*, 29: 25–30.

Ackerson, B. (2003) Coping with the Dual Demands of Severe Mental Illness and Parenting: The Parent's Perspective. *Families in Society*, 84: 109–119.

Aldridge, J. and Becker, S. (2003) *Children Caring for Parents with Mental Illness: Perspectives of Young Carers, Parents and Professionals*, Bristol: Policy Press.

Alston, M. and Kent, J. (2006) *Impact of Drought on Rural and Remote Education Access: A Report to DEST and Rural Education Fund of FRRR*, Wagga: Centre for Rural Social Research.

American Psychiatric Association (2000) *DSM-IV TR-TR Diagnostic & Statistical Manual of Mental Health Disorders*, 4th Edition. Washington, D.C.: University of New South Wales Electronic Resource, Accessed 30 May 2007.

Arskey, H., O'Malley, L., Baldwin, S., Harris, J., Newbronner, E., Hare, P. and Mason, A. (2002) *Services to Support Carers of People with Mental Health Problems: Overview Report*, York, Social Policy Unit: University of York.

Arvidsson, H. (2009) Gender Differences in Needs and Care of Severely Mentally Ill Persons: Findings from a Swedish Cross-Sectional and Longitudinal Study. *International Journal of Social Psychiatry*, Online First, Published on 23 July 2009 as doi 10.1177/0020764009106631. Accessed 3 May 2010.

Australian Bureau of Statistics (ABS) (2005) *Australian Social Trends 2005*, Canberra: Commonwealth of Australia.

Australian Bureau of Statistics (ABS) (2007) *National Survey of Mental Health and Well-Being*, Canberra: ABS.

Australian Bureau of Statistics (ABS) (2009) *Australian Social Trends, Mental Health*, Canberra: Commonwealth of Australia.

Australian Capital Territory (1994) Mental Health (Treatment and Care) Act. Accessed 18 March 2010, http://www.health.act.gov.au.

Australian Institute of Health and Welfare (2008) *Australia's Health 2008*, Canberra: The Australian Government.

Australian Institute of Health and Welfare (2010) *Australia's Health 2010*, Canberra: The Australian Government.

Australians for Native Title and Reconciliation (ANTAR) (2004) *Healing Hands: Indigenous Health Rights Action Kit*. Canberra: ANTAR.

Australian Social Inclusion Board (2010) Social Inclusion in Australia: How Australia is Faring, Australian Bureau of Statistics Survey of Education and Work 2001–2008, Canberra, ASIB.

Bachrach, L. L. (1986) Deinstitutionalization: What Do the Numbers Mean? *Hospital and Community Psychiatry*, 37: 118–119.

Baker, D. and North, K. (1999) Does Employment Improve the Health of Lone Mother? *Social Science and Medicine*, 49: 121–131.

Baker-Miller, J. (1976) *Towards a New Psychology of Women*, Penguin: Harmondsworth.

Banks, S. (2006) *Ethics and Values in Social Work*, 3rd Edition, Basingstoke, Hampshire: Macmillan.

Barbato, A. (1998) Psychiatry in Transition: Outcomes of Mental Health Policy Shift in Italy. *Australian and New Zealand Journal of Psychiatry*, 32, 5: 673–679.

Barker, P. (2000) The Construction of Mind and Madness: From Leonardo to Hearing Voices Network, in P. Barker and C. Stevenson (Eds), *The Construction of Power and Authority in Psychiatry*, Oxford: Butterworth-Heinemann.

Barkley, R. A. (1990) *Attention-Deficit Hyperactivity Disorder: A Handbook for Diagnosis and Treatment*, New York: Guilford Press.

Barkley, R. A. (2000) *Taking Charge of ADHD: The Complete Authoritative Guide for Parents*, New York: Guilford Press.

Barn, R. (2008) Ethnicity, Gender and Mental Health: Social Worker Perspectives. *International Journal of Social Psychiatry*, 54: 69–82.

Barnes, M., Davis, A. and Rogers, H. (2006) Women's Voices, Women's Choices: Experiences and Creativity in Consulting Women Users of Mental Health Services. *Journal of Mental Health*, 5, 3: 329–341.

BBC (2010) http://www.bbc.co.uk/news/education-11757907.

Beddoe, L. and Maidment, J. (2009) Exploring a 'Life-Course' Approach to Practice, in L. Beddow and J. Maidment (Eds), *Mapping Knowledge for Social Work Practice: Critical Intersections*, South Melbourne: Cengage Learning.

Beitchman, J. H., Zucker, K. J., Hood, J. E., da Costa, G. A. and Akman, D. (1991) A Review of the Short-Term Effects of Child Sexual Abuse. *Child Abuse and Neglect*, 10, 4: 537–556.

Bellamy, J. and Cowling, S. (2008) The Lived Experience of Welfare Reform: Stories from the Field, paper presented to ARACY ARC/NHMRC Research Network Supported Workshop on the Impact of Welfare-to-Work and Workplace Reforms on Young People and Children at Risk. University of Sydney, 13 February.

Benner, P. and Wrubel, J. (1989) *The Primacy of Caring: Stress and Coping in Health and Illness*, CA: Addison-Wesley.

Bennett, H. and Hallen. P. (2005) Guardianship and Financial Management Legislation: What Doctors in Aged Care Need to Know. *Internal Medicine Journal*, 35: 482–487.

Bentall, R. P. and Morrison, A. P. (2002) More Harm than Good: The Case Against Using Anti-Psychotic Drugs to Prevent Severe Mental Illness. *Journal of Mental Health*, 11, 4: 351–356.

Beresford, P. (2000) 'Service Users' Knowledges and Social Work Theory: Conflict or Collaboration? *British Journal of Social Work*, 30: 489–503.

Beresford, P. (2006) Developing Inclusive Partnerships: User-defined Outcomes, Networking and Knowledge – A Case Study. *Health and Social Care in the Community*, 14, 5: 436–444.

Bernheim, K. F., Lewine, R. R. and Beale, C. T. (1982) *The Caring Family: Living with Chronic Mental Illness*, New York: Random House.

Beukens, P., Keusch, G., Belizan, J. and Bhutta, Z. A. (2004) Evidence-Based Global Health. *The Journal of the American Medical Association*, 291, 21: 2639–2641.

Bhardwaj, A. (2001) Growing Up Young, Asian and Female in Britain. *Feminist Review*, 68: 52–57.

Biering, P. (2002) Caring for the Involuntarily Hospitalized Adolescent: The Issue of Power in the Nurse-Patient Relationship. *Journal of Child and Adolescent Psychiatric Nursing*, 49, 2: 147–152.

Biggs, S. and Powell, J. L. (2001) A Foucaldian Analysis of Old Age and the Power of Social Welfare, *Journal of Ageing and Social Policy*, 12, 2: 93–112.

Bilsborrow, S. (1992) *You Grow Up Fast As Well: Young Carers on Merseyside*. Barnardos: Carers National Association, Personal Social Services.

Birchwood, M. (2000) Early Intervention and Sustaining the Management of Vulnerability. *Australian and New Zealand Journal of Psychiatry*, 34, 2: 181–184.

Blanchard, M. (2006) Cultural Diversity in Practice: Working with Indigenous People – A Meeting of Minds and Hearts, in A. O'Hara and Z. Weber (Eds), *Skills for Human Service Practice*, South Melbourne: Oxford University Press.

Bland, R., Renouf, N. and Tullgren, A. (2009) *Social Work Practice in Mental Health*, Crows Nest: Allan and Unwin.

Blashfield, R. (1996) Predicting DSM-V. *Journal of Nervous and Mental Disease*, 184: 4–7.

Borrill, J. (2000) *Developments in Treatment of People with Psychotic Experiences*, Updates Vol. 2, Issue 9, London: Mental Health Foundation.

Bourke, L. (2001) One Big Happy Family? Social Problems in Rural Communities, in L. Stewart and L. Bourke (Eds), *Rurality Bites: The*

Social and Environmental Transformation of Rural Australia, Annandale: Pluto Press Australia.

Bourne, H. (1991) The Case for the 'Re-Professionalized' Psychiatrist in Britain, in S. Boyd, C. P. Aisbett, D. L. Francis, K. Kelly, M. Newnham and K. Newnham (Eds), (2006) Issues in Rural Adolescent Mental Health in Australia, *Rural and Remote Health*, 6: 501 (Online).www.rrh.org.au/publishedarticles/article_print_501.pdf Accessed May 27th 2010.

Boyd-Franklin, N. (2003) *Black Families In Therapy: Understanding The African-American Experience*, N.Y: Guilford Press, N.Y.

Boyle, M. (2000) Diagnosis, Science and Power, in P. Barker and C. Stevenson (Eds), *The Construction of Power and Authority in Psychiatry*, Oxford: Butterworth-Heinemann.

Bracken, P. and Thomas, P. (2001) Postpsychiatry: A New Direction for Mental Health. *British Medical Journal*, 24 March, 322, 7288: 724–727.

Bracken, P. and Thomas, P. (2005) *Postpsychiatry: Mental Health in a Postmodern World*, Oxford: Oxford University Press.

Brechin, A. (2000) The Challenge of Caring Relationship, in A. Brechin, H. Brown and M. Eby (Eds), *Critical Practice in Health and Social Care*, London: Sage: 141–163.

Breggin, P. (1979) *Electroshock: Its Brain-Disabling Effects*, New York: Springer.

Breggin, P. (1983) *Psychiatric Drugs: Hazards to the Brain*, New York: Springer.

Breggin, P. (1991) *Toxic Psychiatry*, New York: St. Martin's Press.

Broverman, D., Clarkson, F., Rosencratz, O. et al. (1970) Sex Role Stereoptypes and Clinical Judgements of Mental Health. *Journal of Consulting and Clinical Psychology*, 34: 1–7.

Brown, P. (1990) The Name Game: Towards a Sociology of Diagnosis. *Journal of Mind and Behaviour*, 11: 385–406.

Brown, G. and Moran, P. (1997) Lone Mothers, Poverty and Depression. *Psychological Medicine*, 27: 21–33.

Brown, G. and Harris, T. (1978) *The Social Origins of Depression: A Study of Psychiatric Disorder in Women*, London: Tavistock.

Brown, L. S. (1992) A Feminist Critique of the Personality Disorders, in L. S. Brown and M. Ballou (Eds), *Personality and Psychopathology: Feminist Reappraisals*. New York: Guidford.

Brown, P. (1985) *The Transfer of Care: Psychiatric Deinstitutionalization and Its Aftermath*, Boston: Routledge and Kegan Paul.

Brown, P. (1990) The Name Game: Toward a Sociology of Diagnosis. *Journal of Mind and Behavior*, 11: 385–406.

Buck, M. (1997) The Price of Poverty: Mental Health and Gender. *Critical Social Policy*, 17: 79–97.

Busfield, J. (1996) *Men, Women and Madness*, Basingstoke, Hampshire: Macmillan Press.

Bytheway, B. and Johnson, J. (1998) The Social Construction of 'Carers', in A. Symonds and A. Kelly (Eds), *The Social Construction of Community Care*, Basingstoke, Hampshire: Macmillan Press.

Campbell, P. (1996) User Action – The Last Ten Years. *Mental Health Review Journal*, 1, 4: 14–15.

Cappo, M. D. (2006) Alcohol, Drugs and Mental Health – A Heady Mix: A Joint Forum of the Mental Health Coalition of South Australia and South Australian Network of Drug and Alcohol Services. Accessed 15 January 2009.

Capra, R. (1982) *The Turning Point, Science, Society and the Rising Culture*, London: Wildwood House.

Carney, T. (2008) The Mental Health Service Crisis of Neoliberalism – An Antipodean Perspective. *International Journal of Law and Psychiatry*, 31: 101–115.

Chamberlin, J. (1978) *On Our Own: Patient-Controlled Alternatives to the Mental Health System*, New York: McGraw-Hill.

Chang, K. H. and Horrocks, S. (2006) Lived Experiences of Family Caregivers of Mentally Ill Relatives. *Journal of Advanced Nursing*, 53, 4: 435–443.

Chesler, P. (1972) *Women and Madness*, New York: Doubleday.

Clare, A. (1983) *Psychiatry in Dissent*, London: Tavistock.

Clarke, L. (2004) *The Time of Therapeutic Communities*, London: Jessica Kingsley Publishers.

Coffey, C. E. and Weiner, R. (1990) Electroconvulsive Therapy: An Update. *Hospital and Community Psychiatry*, 41, 5: 515–521.

Coleman, R. (2000) The Politics of Illness, in P. Barker and C. Stevenson (Eds), *The Construction of Power and Authority in Psychiatry*, Oxford: Butterworth-Heinemann.

Coleman, R. (2002) Hearing Voices and the Politics of Oppression, in C. Newnes, G. Holmes and C. Dunn (Eds), *This is Madness*, Llangarron: PCCS Books.

Coleman, J. and Hagell, A. (2007) *Adolescence, Risk and Resilience: Against the Odds*, Chichester: John Wiley and Sons.

Coleman, J. and Schofield, J. (2001) *Key Data on Adolescence*, Brighton: Trust for the Study of Adolescence.

Collins, S. L, Levin, F. R., Foltin, R. W., Kleber, H. D. and Evans S. M. (2006) Response to Cocaine, Alone and in Combination with Methylphenidate in Cocaine Abusers with ADHD. *Drug and Alcohol Dependence*, 82, 2: 158–167.

Committee on the Social Determinants of Health (CSDH) (2008) Closing the Gap in A Generation: Health Equity through Action on the Social Determinants of Health. *Final Report of the Commission on Social Determinants of Health*, Geneva: World Health Organisation.

Commonwealth Department of Health and Ageing (1996) *The National Standards for Mental Health Services*. Canberra, ACT, Australia: Mental Health Branch.

Commonwealth Department of Health and Ageing (2002) *National Practice Standards for the Mental Health Workforce*. Canberra, ACT, Australia: Mental Health Branch.

Commonwealth of Australia (2009) *A Stronger Fairer Australia National Statement on Social Inclusion*, Canberra: Department of Prime Minister and Cabinet.

Commonwealth Department of Health and Ageing (2010) *The Revised National Standards for Mental Health Services*. Canberra, ACT, Australia: Mental Health Branch.

Connell, R. W (2000) *The Men and the Boys*, St Leonards: Allen and Unwin.

Connell, R. W. (2005) *Masculinities*, 2nd Edition, Berkley: University of California Press.

Conrad, P. (2007) *The Lexicalization of Society: On the Transformation of Human Conditions into Treatable Disorders*, Baltimore: John Hopkins University Press.

Cooper, D. (1967) *Psychiatry and Anti-Psychiatry*, London, Paladin.

Coppock, V. and Hopton, J. (2000) *Critical Perspectives on Mental Health*, London: Routledge.

Cornah, D. (2002) *Promoting Engagement Project*, Updates Vol. 3, Issue 16, London: The Mental Health Foundation.

Crotty, M. (1996) *Phenomenology and Nursing Research*, Melbourne: Churchill Livingstone.

Davis, C., Martin, G., Kosky, R., & O'Hanlon, A. (2000). *Early Intervention in the Mental Health of Young People*. Adelaide: Australian Early Intervention Network for Mental Health in Young People.

de Girolamo, G. and Cozza, M. (2000) The Italian Psychiatric Reform. *International Journal of Law and Psychiatry*, 23, 3–4: 197–214.

Deasy, L. C. and Quinn, O. W. (1955) The Wife of the Mental Patient and the Hospital Psychiatrist. *Journal of Social Issues*, 11: 49–60.

Deegan, P. (1988) Recovery: The Lived Experience Rehabilitation. *Psychiatric Rehabilitation Journal*, 11: 11–19.

Department of Health (DOH) (1989) *Caring for People: Community Care in the Next Decade and Beyond*, Cm 849, London: HMSO.

Department of Health (2003) *Mental Health Policy Implementation Guide: Support, Time and Recovery (STR) Workers*, London: The Stationery Office.

Deveson, A. (1991) *Tell Me I'm Here*, Ringwood: Penguin.

Dols, M. W. (1992) *Majnun: The Madman in Medieval Islamic Society*, Oxford: Clarendon Press.

Drake, R., Yovetich, N., Bebout, R., Harris, M. and Mchugo, G. (1997) Integrated Treatment for Dually Diagnosed Homeless Adults. *Journal of Nervous and Mental Disease*, 185, 5: 298–305.

Duncan, S. (1998) The Spatiality of Gender. *Innovation*, 11, 2: 119–128.

Edwards, C. and Imrie, R. (2008) Disability and the Implication of the Wellbeing Agenda: Some Reflections from the United Kingdom. *Journal of Social Policy*, 37, 3: 337–355.

Ehrenreich, B. and English, D. (1973) For Her Own Good, in T. Szasz (Ed.), *In the Age of Madness*, New York: Anchor.

Ehrenreich, B. and English, D. (1978) *For Her Own Good: 150 Years of the Experts' Advice to Women*, New York: Anchor-Doubleday.

Ellenberger, H. F. (1974) Psychiatry from Ancient to Modern Times, in S. Arieti (Ed.), *American Handbook of Psychiatry*, 2nd Edition, New York: Basic Books.

Ellis-Jones, I. (2002) *Accredited Persons under the Mental Health Act 1990 in the Context of Administrative Decision Making*, New South Wales, Australia: New South Wales Institute of Psychiatry.

Emerson, R., Burke Rochford Jr., E. and Shaw, L. (1981) Economics and Enterprise in Board and Care Homes for the Mentally Ill. *American Behavioral Psychologist*, 24: 771–785.

Ensink, T. and Sauer, C. (1993) *Framing and Perspectivising in Discourse*, Amsterdam: John Benjamins Publishing Co.

Evans, J. and Repper, J. (2000) Employment, Social Inclusion and Mental Health. *Journal of Psychiatric and Mental Health Nursing*, 7: 15–24.

Faith, K. (1993) *Unruly Women: The Politics of Confinement and Resistance*, Vancouver: Press Gang Publishers.

Farrington, D. (1994) Human Development and Criminal Careers, in M. Maguire, R. Morgan, and R. Reiner (Eds), *Oxford Handbook of Criminology*, Oxford: Oxford University Press.

Fausto-Sterling, A. (1985) *Myths of Gender*, New York: Basic Books.

Fawcett, B. (2000a) *Feminist Perspectives on Disability*, Harlow: Prentice Hall.

Fawcett, B. (2000b) Researching Disability, in B. Fawcett, B. Featherstone, J. Fook and A. Rossiter (Eds) *Practice and Research in Social Work: Postmodern Feminist Perspectives*, London: Routledge.

Fawcett, B. (2008) Women and Violence, in B. Fawcett and F. Waugh (Eds) *Addressing Violence, Abuse and Oppression*, London and New York: Routledge.

Fawcett, B. (2009) *Day Care, Older People and 'Carers': An Exploratory Study of the Relationship between Day Centre Attendance, Increased Resilience and Improved Health and Psycho-Social Outcomes*, Sydney: University of Sydney.

Fawcett, B. (2011) *Day Care, Older People and Carers: An Exploratory Study of the Relationship between Day Centre Attendance, Increased Resilience and Improved Health and Psychosocial Outcomes*, Research Report produced for UnitingCare, Hammond Care, Catholic Care and the Royal North Shore Hospital Rehabilitation Unit, Sydney, University of Sydney.

Fawcett, B. and Hanlon, B. (2009a) The 'Return To Community': Challenges for Human Service Professionals. *Journal of Sociology*, 45, 4: 433–444.

Fawcett, B. and Hanlon, M. (2009b) Child Sexual Abuse and Aboriginal Communities in Australia: A Case Study of Non-Inclusive Government Intervention. *European Journal of Social Work*, 12, 1: 71–86.

Fawcett, B. and Karban, K. (2005) *Contemporary Mental Health: Theory, Policy and Practice*, London: Routledge.

Fawcett, B. and Reynolds, J. (2010) Mental Health and Older Women: The Challenges for Social Perspectives and Community Capacity Building. *British Journal of Social Work*, 40, 5: 1452–1470.

Fawcett, B., Featherstone, B. and Goddard J. (2004) *Contemporary Child Care Policy and Practice*, Basingstoke, Hampshire: Palgrave Macmillan.

Fawcett, B., Goodwin, S., Meagher, G. and Phillips, R. (2010) *Social Policy for Social Change*, South Yarra: Palgrave Macmillan.

Featherstone. B. (2004) *Family Life and Family Support, a Feminist Analysis*, Basingstoke, Hampshire: Palgrave Macmillan.

Fernando, S. (2002) *Mental Health, Race and Culture*. 2nd Edition, Basingstoke, Hampshire: Palgrave Macmillan.

Fernando, S. (2003) *Cultural Diversity, Mental Health and Psychiatry*, London: Routledge.

Fernando, S., Ndegwa, D. and Wilson, M. (1998) *Forensic Psychiatry, 'Race' and Culture*, London: Routledge.

Flaskenid, J. (1992) Relationship of Ethnicity to Psychiatric Diagnosis. *Journal of Nervous Mental Disease*, 180, 5: 296–303. Williams and Wilkins. Accessed 16 2009.

Fleming, A. S., Klein, E. and Corter, C. (1992) The Effects of a Social Support Group on Depression, Maternal Attitudes and Behaviour in New Mothers. *Journal of Child Psychology and Psychiatry*, 33, 4: 686–698.

Fook, J. (2002) *Social Work: Critical Theory and Practice*, London, Thousand Oaks: Sage.

Fook, J. (2009) *Critical Reflection: Overview and Latest Ideas, AASSWE Workshop*, Melbourne: Monash University.

Foucault, M. (1973) *Madness and Civilization*, New York: Vintage.

Foucault, M. (1977) *Discipline and Punish* (A. Sheridan, Trans.), NewYork: Pantheon Books.

Foucault, M. (1980a) Power and Strategies, in M. Foucault (Ed.) *Power/Knowledge. Selected Interviews and Other Writing*, New York: Pantheon Books.

Foucault, M. (1980b) *Michel Foucault: Power/Knowledge: Selected Interviews and Other Writings 1972–1977* C. Gordon (Ed.) Hemel Hempstead: Harvester Wheatsheaf.

Foucault, N. (1981) Question of Method: An Interview with Michel Foucault. *Ideology and Consciousness*, 8: 1–14.

Fox, R. (1978) *So Far Disordered in Mind*, Berkeley: University of California Press.

Frame, J. (2008) *An Angel at My Table*, Sydney: Random House.

France, A. and Utting, D. (2005) The Paradigm of Risk and Protection Focused Prevention and Its Impact on Services for Children and Families. *Children and Society*, 19, 2: 77–90.

Francis, E. (1988) Black People, Dangerousness and Psychiatric Compulsion, in A. Brachx and C. Grimshaw (Eds), *Mental Health Care in Crisis*, London: Pluto.

Frank, L. R. (1990) Electroshock: Death, Brain Damage, Memory Loss and Brainwashing. *Journal of Mind and Behavior*, 11, 3–4: 489–512.

Fraser, M. and Blishen, S. (2007) *Supporting Young People's Mental Health: Eight Points for Action: A Policy Briefing from the Mental Health Foundation*, London: The Mental Health Foundation.

Friedli, L. (2009) *Mental Health, Resilience and Inequalities*, Copenhagen: WHO.

Gilbert, P. (1998) What Is Shame? Some Core Issues and Controversies, in P. Gilbert and B. Andrews (Eds), *Shame: Interpersonal Psychopathology and Culture*, Oxford: Oxford University Press.

Glaves, A. (2006) Those Labelled 'Mentally Ill' Should Be Helped, Not Forcibly Drugged, Las Cruces Sun-News, New Mexico, USA. Accessed 28 June 2008.

Goffman, E. (1984) *Asylums*, Harmondsworth: Penguin.

Golightley, M. (2006) *Social Work and Mental Health*, Exeter: Learning Matters Ltd.

Golightley, M. (2008) *Social Work and Mental Health*, Exeter: Learning Matters Ltd.

Goodwin, S. (1997) *Comparative Mental Health Policy: From Institutional to Community Care*, London: Sage Publications.

Gorell Barnes, G. (1996) The Mentally Ill Parent and the Family System, in M. Gostin and L. Gable (Eds) (2004) The Human Rights of Persons With Mental Disabilities: A Global Perspective on The Application of Human Rights Principles to Mental Health. *Maryland Law Review*, 63: 20–121.

Graham, H. (1983) Caring: A Labour of Love, in J. Finch and D. Groves (Eds), *A Labour of Love: Women, Work and Caring*, London: Routledge and Kegan Paul.

Graham, L.J. (ed) (2010) *(De) Constructing ADHD: Critical Guidance for Teachers and Teacher Educators*, New York: Peter Lang Publishing.

Gralnick, A. (1985) Build a Better State Hospital: Deinstitutionalization Has Failed. *Hospital and Community Psychiatry*, 36, 7: 738–745.

Gray, B., Robinson, C. A., Seddon, D. and Roberts, A. (2009) An Emotive Subject Insights from Social, Voluntary and Healthcare Professionals into the Feelings of Family Carers for People with Mental Health Problems. *Health and Social Care in the Community*, 17, 2: 125–132.

Green, H., McGinnity, A., Meltzer, A. H., Ford, T. and Goodman, R. (2005) *Mental Health of Children and Young People in Britain 2004*, Basingstoke, Hampshire: Palgrave Macmillan.

Green, L. and Taylor, J. (2010) Exploring the Relationship between Gender and Child Health: A Contemporary Analysis of High and Low Economic Resource Countries, in B. Featherstone, C. Hooper, J. Scourfield and J. Taylor (Eds), *Gender and Child Welfare in Society*, Chichester: Wiley-Blackwell.

Greenberg, M. (2009) *Hurry Down Sunshine*, London: Bloomsbury.

Greenhalgh, T. (1998) Narrative Based Medicine in an Evidence Based World, in T. Greenhalgh and B. Hurwitz (Eds) *Narrative Based Medicine*, London: BMG Books.

Grenier, A. (2004) Older Women Negotiating Uncertainty in Everyday Life: Contesting Risk Management Systems, in L. Davies and P. Leonard (Eds), *Social Work in a Corporate Era: Practices of Power and Resistance*, Birmingham: Ashgate.

Grier, W. H. and Cobbs, P. M. (1969) *Black Rage*, New York: Bantam Books.

Griffith, R. (1988) *Community Care: Agenda for Action, White Paper*, London: HMSO.

Grob, G. N. (1983) *Mental Illness and American Society 1875–1940*, Princeton: Princeton University Press.

Grob, G. N. (2008) Mental Health Policy in the Liberal State: The Example of The United States. *International Journal of Law and Psychiatry*, 31: 89–100.

Gureje, O. and Alem, A. (2000) Mental Health and Policy Development in Africa. *Bulletin of the World Health Organization*, 78, 4: 475–482.

Guze, S. (1989) Biological Psychiatry: Is There Any Other Kind? *Psychological Medicine*, 19, 2: 314–322.

Hall, W. (1996) What Have Population Surveys Revealed About Substance Use Disorders and Their Co-Morbidity with Other Mental Disorders? *Drug and Alcohol Review*, 15, 157–170.

Hancock, L. (2001) The Care Crunch: Changing Work, Families and Welfare in Australia. *Critical Social Policy*, 21, 1, 119–140.

Hanlon, M. (2008) Men and Violence, in B. Fawcett and F. Waugh (Eds) *Addressing Violence, Abuse and Oppression: Debates and Challenges*, London and New York: Routledge.

Hanlon, P. and Taylor, A. (2002) *Personal Participation Plans. Mental Health Matters.* Winter edition 17–22, New South Wales, Australia: The Mental Health Association.

Hare-Mustin, R. T. (1983) An Appraisal of the Relationship between Women and Psychotherapy – 80 Years after the Case of Dora. *American Psychologist,* 38: 593–601.

Hatfield, A. B. and Lefley, H. P. (1993) *Surviving Mental Illness,* New York: The Guildford Press.

Hatfield, A. B. (1997) *Families of the Mentally Ill: Coping and Adaptation,* New York: Guilford.

Hauck, Y., Rock, D., Jackiewicz, T. and Jablensky, A. (2008) Healthy Babies for Mothers with Serious Mental Illness: A Case Management Framework for Mental Health Clinicians. *International Journal of Mental Health Nursing,* 17, 383–391.

Hazelton, M. (2005) Mental Health Reform, Citizenship and Human Rights in Four Countries. *Health Sociology Review,* 14, 3: 230–241.

Hazelton, M. and Clinton, M. (2002) Mental Health Consumers Or Citizens With Mental Health Problems?, in S. Henderson and A. Petersen (Eds) *Consuming Health,* London: Routledge.

Hazelton, M. and Clinton, M. (2004) Human Rights, Citizenship and Mental Health Reform in Australia, in P. Morrall and M. Hazelton (Eds) *Mental Health: Global Policies and Human Rights,* London: Whurr.

Healy, K. (2009) A Case of Mistaken Identity: The Social Welfare Professions and New Public Management. *Journal of Sociology,* 45, 4: 383–400.

Hearn, J. (2005) Autobiography, Nation, Postcolonialism and Gender Relations: Reflecting on Men in England, *Finland and Ireland, Irish Journal of Sociology,* 14, 2: 66–93.

Heller, J. (1961) *Catch-22,* New York: Simon and Schuster.

Heyman (Ed.) (1998) *Risks, Health and Health Care,* London: Arnold.

Hooley, J. (1985) Expressed Emotion: A Review of the Critical Literature. *Clinical Psychology Review,* 5, 2: 119–139.

Hoppe, R. B. (1985) The Case for or Against Diagnostic and Therapeutic Sexism, in C.T. Mowbray, S. Lanir and M. Hulce (Eds) *Women and Mental Health,* New York: Harrington Park Press.

Horwitz, A. (2002) *Creating Mental Illness,* Chicago: The University of Chicago Press.

Horwitz, A., Tessler, R., Fisher, G. and Gamache, G. (1992) The Role of Adult Siblings in Providing Support to the Seriously Mentally Ill. *Journal of Marriage and Family,* 54: 233–241.

House, J.S., Robbins, C. and Metzner, H.L. (1982) The Association of Social Relationships and Activities with Mortality: Prospective Evidence From The Tecumseh Community Health Study, *American Journal of Epidemiology,* 116, 1: 123–140.

Howard, L., Shah, N., Salmon, M. and Appleby, L. (2003) Predictors of Social Services Supervision of Babies of Mothers with Mental Illness after Admission to a Psychiatric Mother and Baby Unit. *Social Psychiatry and Psychiatric Epidemiology*, 38: 450–455.

Howarth, C. and Street, C. (2000) *Sidelined: Young Adults' Access to Services*, London: New Policy Institute.

Howie, L., Coulter, M. and Feldman, S. (2004) Crafting the Self: Older Persons Narratives of Occupational Identity. *The American Journal of Occupational Therapy*, 58: 446–454. http://www.facsia.gov.au. Accessed February 2008.

Hughes, J.C., Louw, S.J. and Sabat, S.R. (ed.) (2006) *Dementia: Mind, Meaning and the Person*, Oxford: Oxford University Press.

Hughes, J.C. (2011) *Thinking Through Dementia*, Oxford: Oxford University Press.

Jablensky, A., Sartorius, N., Ernberg, G., Anker, M., Korten, A., Cooper, J. E., Day, R. and Bertelsen, A. (1991) Schizophrenia: Manifestations, Incidence, and Course in Different Cultures (World Health Organization Ten Country Study). *Psychological Medicine*, Monograph Supplement 20, Cambridge: Cambridge University Press.

James, A. M. (2007) Principles of Youth Participation in Mental Health Services. *The Medical Journal of Australia, Consumer Perspectives*, 187, 7, October, 2007: 57–60.

Jeffrey C. and McDonnell, L. (2004) Youth in a Comparative Perspective: Global Change, Local Lives. *Youth and Society*, 36, 2: 131–142.

Jenkins, R. (2005) Mental Health in Post Communist Countries. *BMJ Helping Doctors Make Better Decisions*, 331: 173–174. Accessed 4 July 2008.

Jimenez, M. A. (1997) Gender and Psychiatry: Psychiatric Conceptions of Mental Disorders In Women, 1960–1994. *Affilia*, 12: 154–175.

Johnson, Z., Molloy, B., Scallen, F., Fitzpatrick, R. B., Keegan, T. and Byre, P. (2000) Community Mothers Programme – Seven Year Follow up of a Randomized Controlled Trial of Non Professional Intervention in Parenting. *Journal of Public Health Medicine*, 22, 3: 337–342.

Jones, K. (1988) *Experience in Mental Health*, London: Sage.

Jones, D. W. (2002) *Myths, Madness and the Family*, Basingstoke, Hampshire: Palgrave Macmillan.

Jukes, L. and McLaughlin, J. (2005) Outpatient Group Treatment Program for Co-morbid Psychosis and Substance Abuse. 15th Annual Themes Conference, Australia.

Kaplan, M. (1988) A Woman's View of DSM-III. *American Psychologist*, 38, 7: 786–792.

Kaysen, S. (2000) *Girl, Interrupted*, London: Virago.

Keith, C. (1995) Family Caregiving Systems: Models, Resources and Values. *Journal of Marriage and the Family*, 57, February: 179–189.

Kenny, A., Kidd, S., Tuena, J., Jarius, M. and Robertson, A. (2006) Falling through the Cracks: Supporting Young People with Dual Diagnosis in Rural and Regional Victoria. *Australian Journal of Primary Health*, 12, 3 : 12–19.

Kessler, R. C., McGonagh, K. A., Zhao, S., Nelson, C. B., Hughes, M., Eshlemon, S., Wittchen, U. and Kendler, K. S. (1994), Lifetime and 12 Month Prevalence of DSM-11-R Psychiatric Disorders in the United States. *Archives of General Psychiatry*, 51: 8–19.

Kitwood, T. (1997) *Dementia Reconsidered: The Person Comes First*, Buckingham: Open University Press.

Koppelman, E. R. (2002) Dementia and Dignity: Towards a New Method of Surrogate Decision Making. *The Journal of Medicine and Philosophy*, 27, 1: 65–85.

Kuno, E. and Asukai, N. (2000) Efforts toward Building a Community-Based Mental Health System in Japan. *International Journal of Law and Psychiatry*, 23, 3–4: 361–373.

Kurtz, Z. (2003) Outcomes for Children's Health and Well-Being. *Children and Society*, 17: 173–183.

La Fond, J. and Srebnik, D. (1999) The Impact ff Mental Health Advance Directives on Patient Perceptions of Coercion in Civil Commitment and Treatment Decision. *International Journal of Law and Psychiatry*, 2002, 50, 7: 919–925. Accessed 30 May 2008.

Lagan, M., Knights, K., Barton, J. and Boyce, P. M. (2009) Advocacy for Mothers with Psychiatric Illness: A Clinical Perspective. *International Journal of Mental Health Nursing*, 18: 53–61.

Laing, R. D. (1959) *The Divided Self*, Harmondsworth: Penguin.

Laing, R. D. (1967) *The Politics of Experience*, New York: Ballantine.

Laing, R. D. (1982) *The Voice of Experience*, New York: Pantheon.

Lamb, H. R. and Bachrach, L. L. (2001) Some Perspectives on Deinstitutionalization. *Psychiatric Services*, 52, 8: 1039–1045.

Lawton-Smith (2006) Compulsory Treatment Orders: Lessons from Scotland, King's Fund. Accessed 19 March 2010.

Leff, J. (1988) *Psychiatry around the Globe*, 2nd Edition, London: Gaskell.

Lefley, H. P. (1987a) Impact of Mental Illness in Families of Mental Health Professionals. *Journal of Nervous and Mental Disease*, 175: 613–619.

Lefley, H. P. (1987b) Culture and Mental Illness: The Family Role, in A. B. Hatfield and H. P. Lefley (Eds), *Families of the Mentally Ill: Meeting the Challenges*, San Francisco: Jossey-Bass.

Lefley, H. P. (1990) Culture and Chronic Mental Illness. *Hospital and Community Psychiatry*, 41: 277–286.

Leggatt, M. (2007) Families and Other Carers, in G. Meadows, B. Singh and M. Grigg (Eds), *Mental Health in Australia: Collaborative Community Practice*, South Melbourne: Oxford University Press.

Leonard, R. and Johansson, S. (2008) Policy and Practices Relating to the Active Engagement of Older People in the Community: A Comparison of Sweden and Australia. *International Journal of Social Welfare* 17: 37–45.

Lester, H. and Glasby, J. (2006) *Mental Health Policy and Practice*, Basingstoke, Hampshire: Palgrave Macmillan.

Levy, F., Hay, D. and Bennet K. (2006) Genetics of Attention Deficit Hyperactivity Disorder: A Current Review and Future Prospects. *International Journal of Disability, Development and Education*, 53, 1: 5–20.

Lewis, B. E. (2006) *The Birth of Postpsychiatry*, Michigan: University of Michigan Press.

Lewis, L. (2009) Politics Of Recognition: What Can a Human Rights Perspective Contribute To Understanding Users' Experiences of Involvement in Mental Health Services? *Social Policy and Society*, 8, 2: 257–274.

Link, B. J. and Phelan, J. C. (2001) Conceptualising Stigma. *Annual Review of Sociology*, 27: 363–385.

Lister, R. (2002) The Dilemmas of Pendulum Politics: Balancing Paid Work, Care and Citizenship. *Economy and Society*, 31, 4: 520–532.

Littlewood, R. (1992) Psychiatric Diagnosis and Racial Bias: Empirical and Interpretative Approaches. *Social Science and Medicine*, 34, 2: 141–149.

Lyyra, T. M. and Heikkinen, R. L. (2006) Perceived Social Support and Mortality in Older People. *The Journals of Gerontology*, Series B., *Psychological Sciences and Social Sciences*, Washington, May, 61B, 3: 147–151.

MacDonald, R. (2007) Social Exclusion, Risk and Young Adulthood, in J. Coleman and A. Hagell (Eds), *Adolescence, Risk and Resilience: Against the Odds*, Chichester: John Wiley and Sons: 143–164.

Manthorpe, J. and Iliffe, S. (2005) *Adults in Later Life with Mental Health Problems, Mental Health Foundation*. 3rd Edition, Oxford: Oxford University Press.

Mares, S., Newman, L. and Warren, B. (2005) *Clinical Skills in Infant Mental Health*, N.S.W: Australian Council for Education Research Press.

Marlowe, J. (1996) Helpers, Helplessness and Self-Help: 'Shaping the Silence': A Personal Account, in M. Gopfert, J. Webster and M. V. Seeman (Eds), *Parental Psychiatric Disorder*, Cambridge: Cambridge University Press.

Marsh, D. (1992) *Families and Mental Illness: New Directions in Professional Practice*, New York: Praeger.

Martin, A. J. and Marsh, H. W. (2006) Academic Resilience and its Psychological and Educational Correlates: A Construct Validity Approach. *Psychology in the Schools*, 43: 413–430.

Masson, J. (1988) *Against Therapy*, London: Fontana.

Maurin, J. T. and Boyd, C. B. (1990) Burden of Mental Illness on the Family: A Critical Review. *Archives of Psychiatric Nursing*, 4, 2: 99–107.

McGorry, P. and Yung, A. (2003) Early Intervention in Psychosis: An Overdue Reform: An Introduction to the Early Psychosis Symposium Australia and New Zealand. *Journal of Psychiatry*, 37: 393–8

McGorry, P. D., Parker, A. and Purcell, R. (2007) Youth Mental Health: A New Stream of Mental Health Care for Adolescents and Young Adults, in G. Meadows, B. Singh and M. Grigg (Eds), *Mental Health in Australia*, Melbourne: Oxford University Press.

McLeod, J. (1991) Childhood Parental Loss and Adult Depression. *Journal of Health and Social Behaviour*, 32: 205–220.

Meleis, A. I. and Inn, E. (2002) Grandmothers and Women's Health: From Fragmentation to Coherence. *Health Care for Women International*, 23: 207–224.

Meltzer, H., Gatward, R., Goodman, R. and Ford, T. (2000) *Mental Health of Children and Adolescents in Great Britain: A Survey, 1999 Social Survey Division of ONS*, London: TSO.

Mental Health America (2008) Fact Sheet Dual Diagnosis. Accessed 31 October 2008.

Mental Health Council of Australia (2005) *'Not for Service Report' in Association with the Brain and Mind research Institute and the Human Rights and Equal Opportunities Commission*, Canberra: MHCA.

Mental Health Foundation (2001) *Turned Upside Down: Developing Community Based Crisis Services for 16–25 Year Olds Experiencing a Mental Health Crisis*, London: MHF.

Mental Health Foundation (2004) *No Help in a Crisis – Developing Mental Health Service that Meet Young People's Needs*, London: MHF.

Mental Health Foundation (2005) *Lifetime Impacts: Childhood and Adolescent Mental Health, Understanding The Lifetime Impacts*, London: MHF.

Mental Health Foundation (2009a) Mental Health, Resilience and Inequalities, WHO/Mental Health Foundation – Written by Lynne Friedli and MH Foundation Supported by NIMHE CPAG and Faculty of Public Health www.mentalhealth.org.uk/publications. Accessed 12 June 2009.

Mental Health Foundation (2009b) Statistics on Mental Health http://www.mentalhealth.org.uk/information/mental-health-overview/statistics/. Accessed 12 May 2009.

Mickel, A. (2008) Will Carers be Involved in Compulsory Treatment Orders. Community Care. Co.UK. Accessed 2 July 2009.

Millett, K. (1974) *Flying*, London: Alfred A. Knopf.

Mills, S. and Frost, N. (2007) Growing Up in Substitute Care: Risk and Resilience Factors for Looked-after Young People and Care Leavers', in A. Milne, E. Hatzidimitriadou, and J. Wiseman (Eds), Health and Quality of Life among Older People in Rural England: Exploring the Impact and Efficacy of Policy, *Journal of Social Policy*, 36, 3: 477–495.

Milne, A. Hatzidimitriadou, E. and Wiseman, J. (2007) Health and Quality of Life among Older People in Rural England: Exploring the Impact and Efficacy of Policy. *Journal of Social Policy*, 36, 3: 477–495.

Mindframe (2009) Supported by the Australian Government Department of Health and Ageing. http: www.mindframe.media.info//site/index.cfm?display=86529 Accessed 12 May 2009.

Mindframe (2010) Supported by the Australian Government Department of Health and Ageing. http://www.mindframe-media.info/site/index.cfm?display=84363# Accessed 29 April 2010.

Minkoff, K. (1989) An Integrated Treatment Model for Dual Diagnosis of Psychosis and Addiction. *Hospital and Community Psychiatry*, 40, 10: 1031–1036.

Mission Australia (2009a) *In Their Own Words: Insights Into The Concerns of Young Australians*, Snapshot, Sydney: Macquarie Group Foundation.

Mission Australia (2009b) *The Experiences of Young People. How Do Their Living Arrangements Impact?* Snapshot, Sydney: Macquarie Group Foundation.

Mission Australia (2011) *The Cares and Concerns of Vulnerable Young People*, Snapshot 2011, Sydney: Macquarie Group Foundation.

Mohr, W. K. (1999) Deconstructing the Language of Psychiatric Hospitalization. *Journal of Advanced Nursing*, 29, 5: 1052–1059.

Morrall, P. and Hazelton, M. (Eds) (2004) *Mental Health Global Policies and Human Rights*, London: Whurr (Health Sciences 362.2) Good for an international focus, including Egypt, Italy, India, Russia.

Morris, J. (1993) *Pride against Prejudice*, London: Women's Press.

Morris, J. (1996) *Encounters with Strangers: Feminism and Disability*, London: Women's Press.

Morrow, M. (2006) Women's Voices Matter: Creating Women-Centered Mental Health Policy, in M. Morrow, O. Hankivsky and C. Varcoe (Eds), *Women's Health in Canada. Critical Perspectives on Theory and Policy*. Toronto, ON: University of Toronto Press.

Mueser, K. T., Bond, G. R. and Drake, R. E. (1998) Models of Community Care for Severe Mental Illness: A Review of Research on Case Management. *Schizophrenia Bulletin*, 24: 37–74.

Muir Gray, J. A. (1999) Postmodern Medicine. *Lancet*, 354: 1550–1553.

Munk-Jorgensen, P. (1999) Has Deinstitutionalization Gone Too Far? *European Archives of Psychiatry and Clinical Neuroscience*, 249, 3: 136–143.

Murray, L. (1992) The Impact of Postnatal Depression on Infant Development. *Journal of Child Psychology and Psychiatry*, 33: 543–561.

Murray, P. (2000) Disabled Children, Parents and Professionals: Partnership on Whose Terms? *Disability and Society*, 15, 4: 683–698.

Mussell, B., Cardiff, K. and White, J. (2004) The Mental Health and Well-Being of Aboriginal Children and Youth Guidance for New Approaches and Services: A Research Report Prepared for the British Columbia Ministry of Children and Family Development, Vol 1, Report 9, University of British Columbia: Children's Mental Health Policy Research Programme.

New South Wales Health (2000) The Management of People with Co-Existing Mental Health and Substance use Disorder Discussion Paper New South Wales Health Department: NSW, Australia.

New South Wales Health (2004) *Privacy Legislation*, New South Wales: Health Department.

New South Wales Health (2006) *Drug and Alcohol Plan 2006–2010*, New South Wales: Health Department.

New South Wales Health and New South Wales Police (2007) Memorandum of Understanding between New South Wales Health and the New South Wales Police Service, Australia. Accessed 30 March 2009.

New South Wales Health (2007) The New South Wales Mental Health Act, New South Wales, Australia.

Newnes, C. (2002) Histories of Psychiatry, in C. Newnes, G. Holmes and C. Dunn (Eds), *This is Madness*, Llangarron: PCCS Books.

The NHS Confederation (2009) Key Facts and Trends in Mental Health, Accessed 28 March 2010 http://www.nhsconfed.org

Nicholson, J., Sweeney, E. and Geller, J. (1998) Mothers with Mental Illness: The Competing Demands of Parenting and Living with a Mental Illness. *Psychiatric Services*, 49: 643–649.

Northern Sydney Central Coast Mental Health Services (2007) Memorandum of Understanding between Northern Sydney Central Coast Mental Health Services, Central Coast Sector and Hunter Region Central Coast Office and Department of Ageing Disability and Home Care (DADHC) Community Support Team: Australia.

Northern Territory Government (1998) Mental Health and Related Services Act.http://www.health.nt.gov.au. Accessed 18 March 2010.

Novara, R. (1985) Women and Mental Health: A Community Viewpoint, in C.T. Mowbray, S. Lanir and M. Hulce (Eds), *Women and Mental Health New York: Harrington*, New York: Park Press.

Nygren, B., Alex, L., Jonsen, E., Gustafson, Y., Norberg, A. and Lindman, B. (2005) Resilience, Sense Of Coherence, Purpose in Life and Self Transcendence in Relation to Perceived Physical and Mental Health Amongst the Oldest Old. *Ageing and Mental Health*, 9, 4, July: 354–362.

Oates, M. (1996) Postnatal Mental Illness: Its Importance and Management, in M. Gopfert, J. Webster and M. V. Seeman (Eds), *Parental Psychiatric Disorder*, Cambridge: Cambridge University Press.

Office for National Statistics (2010) *Social Trends*, Basingstoke: Palgrave Macmillan.

Oliver, M. (1983) *Social Work with Disabled People*, Basingstoke, Hampshire: Palgrave Macmillan.

Oliver, M. (1990) *The Politics of Disablement*, Basingstoke, Hampshire: Palgrave Macmillan.

Oliver, M. (1996) *Understanding Disability: From Theory to Practice*, Basingstoke, Hampshire: Palgrave Macmillan.

Oliver, M. and Sapey, B. (2006) *Social Work with Disabled People*, Basingstoke, Hampshire: Palgrave Macmillan.

Olsson, C., Bond, L., Burns J., Vella-Brodrick, D. and Sawyer, S. (2003) Adolescent Resilience: A Concept Analysis. *Journal of Adolescence*, 26: 1–11.

Olweus, D. (1995) Bullying or Peer Abuse at School: Facts And Interventions. *Current Directions in Psychological Science*, 4: 196–2000.

Onyx, J. and Warburton, J. (2003) Volunteering and Health Among Older People: A Review, Australasian, *Journal on Aging*, 22, 2: 65–69.

Parker, R. A. (1981) Tending and Social Policy, in E. M. Goldberg and S. Hatch (Eds) *A New Look at the Personal Social Services*, London: Policy Studies Institute.

Patel, V. (2007) Mental Health of Young People: A Global Public Health Challenge, *The Lancet*, 369, 9569: 1302–1313.

Payne, S. (1999) Outside the Walls of The Asylum? Psychiatric Treatment in the 1980s and 1990s, in P. Bartlett and D. Wright (Eds), *Outside the Walls of the Asylum: The History of Care in the Community, 1750–2000*, London: Athlone Press.

Pease, B. (2003) Men and masculinities: Profeminist approaches to changing men, in J. Allan, B. Pease and L. Briskman (Eds), *Critical Social Work*, London, Allen and Unwin.

Pejiert, A. (2001) Being a Parent of an Adult Son Or Daughter With Severe Mental Illness Receiving Professional Care: Parents' Narratives. *Health and Social Care in the Community*, 9, 4: 194–204.

Perkins, R. and Repper, J. (1999) *Working Alongside People with Long Term Mental Health Problems*, Cheltenham: Stanley Thornes.

Petersen, I., Jeppesen, P., Thorup, A., Abe, I. M, Ohlenschlaeger, J., Christensen, T., Krarup, G, Jorgensen, P. and Nordentoft, M. (2005) A Randomised Multicentre Trial of Integrated Versus Standard Treatment for Patients with a First Episode of Psychotic Illness. *British Medical Journal*, 331: doi.1136/bmj.38565.415000.EOI

Pilgrim, D. and Rogers, A. (1999) *A Sociology of Mental Health and Illness*, 2nd Edition, Buckingham: Open University Press.

Platt, S. (1985) Measuring the Burden of Psychiatric Illness on the Family: An Evaluation of Some Rating Scales. *Psychological Medicine*, 15: 383–393.

Polt, R. (1999) *Heidegger: An Introduction*, London: UCL Press.

Porter, R. (1987) *A Social History of Madness*, London: Phoenix.

Porter, R. (1999) *A Social History of Madness: Stories of the Insane*, London: Orion Books.

Porter, R. and Wright, D. (2003) *The Confinement of The Insane: International Perspectives 1800–1965*, Cambridge: Cambridge University Press.

Pound, A. (1996) Parental Affective Disorder and Childhood Disturbance, in M. Gopfert, J. Webster and M. V. Seeman (Eds), *Parental Psychiatric Disorder*, Cambridge: Cambridge University Press.

Prince, R. and Tcheng-Larouche, F. (1987) Culture-Bound Syndromes and International Disease Classifications. *Culture, Medicine and Psychiatry*, 11: 3–19.

Prior, D. (1993) *Social Organization of Mental Illness*, London: Sage.

Prior, P. and Hayes, B. (2001) Changing places: Men Replace Women in Mental Health Beds in Britain. *Social Policy and Administration*, 35, 4: 397–410.

Prior, P. M. (1999) *Gender and Mental Health*, Basingstoke, Hampshire: Macmillan.

Queensland Government (2000) Mental Health Act. http://www.health. qld.gov.au. Accessed 18 March 2010.

Queensland Government (2003) Guidelines for Collaboration between Queensland Health – Mental Health Services Disability Services Queensland and Funded Disability Services Providers in the Provision of Services to People with a Dual Diagnosis of Intellectual Disability and Mental Disorder/Illness. Accessed 30 May 2007.

Raphael, D. (2004) *Social Determinants of Health. Canadian Perspectives*, Toronto, ON: Canadian Scholars' Press Inc.

Rayner, M. and Montague, M. (2000) Resilient Children and Young People: A Discussion Paper Based on a Review of the International Research Literature, Policy and Practice Research Unit, Melbourne: Children's Welfare Association of Victoria.

Rees, N. (2003) International Human Rights and Mental Health Review Tribunal Obligations. *Psychiatry, Psychology and He Law*, 10, 1: 33–43.

Rees, S. (1991) *Achieving Power: Practice and Policy in Social Welfare*, Crows Nest: Allen and Unwin.

Reis, R. (1992) Serial, Parallel and Integrated Models of Dual-Diagnosis Treatment. *Journal of Health Care for the Poor and Undeserved*, 3, 1: 173–181.

Reupert, A. and Maybery, D. (2007) Families Affected by Parental Mental Illness: A Multiperspective Account of Issues and Interventions. *American Journal of Orthopsychiatry*, 77: 362–369.

Rhodes, A. E., Goering, P. N., To, T. and Williams, J. I. (2002) Gender and Outpatient Mental Health Service Use. *Social Science and Medicine*, 54, 1, 1–10.

Rice, S. (1988) *Some Doctors Make You Sick*, Sydney: Angus and Robertson.

Richmond, D. (2003) Out of the Darkness into the Light – The Richmond Report – Speech Notes. Accessed 30 September 2008.

Ridgely, S., Goldman, H. and Willenberg, M. (1990) Barriers to the Care of Persons with Dual Diagnosis: Organizational and Financing Issues. *Schizophrenia Bulletin*. 16, 1: 125.

Ripa, Y. (1990) *Women and Madness*, Cambridge: Polity Press.

Robinson, E. A. R. (1996) Causal Attributions about Mental Illness: Relationship to Family Functioning. *American Journal of Orthopsychiatry*, 66, 2: 282–295.

Rodgers, H. (1990) *Poor Women, Pool Families: The Economic Plight of America's Female-Headed Household*, New York: M. E. Sharpe Inc.

Rogers, A. and Pilgrim, D. (2001) *Mental Health Policy in Britain*, London, Palgrave Macmillan.

Romme, M. and Escher, S. (1993) *Accepting Voices*, London: MIND.

Roof, W.C. (2001) *Spiritual Marketplace: Baby Boomers and the Remaking of American Religion*, Princeton: Princeton University Press.

Rose, L. (1998) Benefits and Limitations of Professional-Family Interactions: The Family Perspective. *Archives of Psychiatric Nursing*, 12, 3: 140–147.

Rosenthal, E. and Sundram, C. (2004) *The Role of International Human Rights in National Mental Health Legislation*, Geneva: WHO.

Roulstone, A. and Morgan, H. (2009) Neo-Liberal Individualism or Self Directed Support: Are We All Speaking the Same Language on Modernizing Adult Social Care? *Social Policy and Society*, 8, 3: 333–345.

Rowling, L. (2006) Adolescents and Emerging Adulthood (12–17 years and 18–24 years), in M. Cattan and S. Tilford (eds.) *Mental Health Promotion: A Lifespan Approach*, 1: 100–136, Maidenhead, UK: Open University Press.

Rowling, L. and Taylor, A. (2005) Intersectoral Approaches to Promoting Mental Health, in H. Herman, S. Saxena, Rowling, L. (2006) *Mental Health Promotion. A Lifespan Approach, Maidenhead*, England: Open University Press.

Russell, D. (1995) *Women, Madness and Medicine*, Cambridge: Polity Press.

Sabat, S. R. (2002) Surviving Manifestations of Self-Hood in Alzheimer's Disease: A Case Study. *Dementia*, 1, 1: 25–36.

Sadowski, H., Ugarte, B., Kolvin, L., Kaplan, C. and Barnes, J. (1999) Early Life Family Disadvantages and Major Depression in Adulthood. *British Journal of Psychiatry*, 174: 112–120.

Sainsbury Centre for Mental Health (2002) *Breaking the Circles of Fear*. London: SCMH.

Samson, C. (1995) Madness and Psychiatry, in B.S. Turner (Ed.) *Medical Power and Social Knowledge*, 2nd Edition, London: Sage.

Samuels, Z. (2008) Report Condemns Accident and Emergency Departments, 'Sporadic' Mental Health Care, Black Mental Health. United Kingdom. Accessed 30 September 2008.

Sartorius, N. (1997) Fighting Schizophrenia and Its Stigma. A New World Psychiatric Association Educational Programme. *British Journal of Psychiatry*, 170, 297; doi: 10.1192/bjp.170.4.297.

Sawicki, J. (1991) *Disciplining Foucault, Feminism, Power and the Body*, London: Routledge.

Sawyer, M. G., Arney, F. M., Baghurst, P. A., Clark, J. J., Graetz, B. W., Kosky, R. J., Norcombe, B., Patton, G. C., Prior, M. R., Raphael, J. M., Whaites, L. C. and Zubrick, S. R. (2001) The Mental Health of Young People in Australia: Key Findings from the Child and Adolescent Component of the National Survey of Mental Health and Well Being. *Australian and New Zealand Journal of Psychiatry*, December, 35, 6: 806–814.

Sayce, L. (2001) Social Inclusion and Mental Health. *Psychiatric Bulletin*, 25: 121–123.

Sayce, L. (2000) *From Psychiatric Patient to Citizen (Overcoming Discrimination and Social Exclusion)*, Basingstoke, Hampshire: Palgrave Macmillan.

Schepper-Hughes, N. and Lovell, A. M. (1986) Breaking the Circuit Of Social Control: Lessons in Public Psychiatry from Italy and Franco Basaglia. *Social Science and Medicine*, 23, 2: 159–178.

Scheyett, A. M. and McCarthy, E. (2006) Women and Men With Mental Illness: Voicing Different Service Needs. *Affilia*, 21: 407–418.

Schon, D. (1983) *The Reflective Practitioner: How Professionals Think in Action*, London: Temple Smith.

Scull, A. (1977) *De-Carceration: Community Treatment and The Deviant – A Radical View*, Englewood-Cliffs, NJ: Prenctice-Hall.

Scull, A. (1979) *Museums of Madness*, Harmondsworth: Penguin.

Scull, A. (1981) (Ed.), *Madhouses, Mad-Doctors and Madmen*, London: Athlone.

Seeman, T. E., Singer B. H., Ryff, C. D., Dienberg Love, G. and Levy-Storms, L. (2002) Social Relationships, Gender and Allostatic Load across Two Age Cohorts. *Psychosomatic Medicine*, 64, 3, May/June 2002: 395–406.

Selikowitz, M. (2004) *Adhd; The Facts, All the Information You Need Straight from The Experts*, Oxford: Oxford University Press.

Shakespeare, T. (1994) Cultural Representation of Disabled People: Dustbins for Disavowel, *Disability and Society*, 9, 3: 283–299.

Shakespeare, T. (1999) When Is a Man Not a Man? When He Is Disabled, in J. Wild (Ed.), *Working with Men for Change*, London: UCL Press.

Sharma, S. (2003) Human Rights of Mental Patients in India: A Global Perspective. *Current Opinion in Psychiatry*, 16, 5: 547–551.

Sheppard, M. (2002) Mental Health and Social Justice: Gender, Race and Psychological Consequences of Un Fairness. *British Journal of Social Work*, 32: 779–797.

Shonkoff, J. (2005) The Science of Early Childhood Development: Closing the Gap between What We Know and What We Do, Address to Harvard Graduate School of Education, October.

Shorter, E. (2006) The Historical Development of Mental Health Services in Europe, in M. Knapp, D. McDaid, E. Mossialos and G. Thornicroft (Eds) *Mental Health Policy and Practice Across Europe*, London: McGraw-Hill.

Showalter, E. (1985) *The Female Malady: Women, Madness and English Culture, 1830–1980*, New York: Penguin.

Showalter, E. (1987) *The Female Malady: Women, Madness and English Culture, 1830–1980*, London: Virago.

Shucksmith, Mark (2004) Young People and Social Exclusion in Rural Areas. *Sociologia Ruralis*, 44/1: 43–59.

Skolbekken, J. A. (2008) Unlimited Medicalization? Risk and Pathologization of Normality, in A. Petersen and I. Wilkinson, (Eds) *Health, Risk and Vulnerability*, London: Routledge.

Skultans, V. (1979) *English Madness, Ideas on Insanity, 1850–1890*, London: Routledge and Kegan Paul.

Social Exclusion Unit (2005) Transitions Young Adults with Complex Needs, www.socialexclusionunit.gov.uk/download.asp?id=785. A Social Exclusion Unit Final Report, London: Cabinet Office.

Social Trends (2002) *National Statistic Social Trends* No 32 2002 Edition, London: The Stationery Office.

Spandler, H. and Carlton, C. (2009) Psychosis and Human Rights: Conflicts in Mental Health Policy and Practice. *Social Policy and Society*, 8, 2: 245–256.

Spandler, H. and Carlton, T. (2009) Psychosis and Human Rights: Conflicts in Mental Health Policy and Practice. *Social Policy and Society*, 8, 2: 245–257.

Spector, R. E. (2003) *Cultural Diversity in Health and Illness* (6th Edition), Upper Saddle River, NJ: Prentice-Hall.

Srebnik, D. S. and Kim, S. Y. (2006) Competency for Creation, Use and Revocation of Psychiatric Advance Directives. *Head Psychiatry Law*, 34, 4: 501–561.

Stanley N. and Manthorpe, J. (2008) Small Acts of Care: Exploring the Potential Impact of the Mental Capacity Act 2005 (UK) On Day-To-Day Support. *Social Policy and Society*, 8, 1: 37–48.

State Government of Victoria (2008) Mental Health Responses in Emergency Departments, Department of Human Services. Victoria. Accessed 30 September 2008.

State Government of Victoria (2010) Better Health Channel: Dual Diagnosis, http://health.vic.gov.au/bharticles.nsf/pages/Dual Diagnosis. Accessed 21 July 2011.

Stefan, S. (2006) Emergency Department Assessment of Psychiatric Patients: Reducing Inappropriate Inpatient Admissions. Medscape. Accessed 30 September 2008.

Steinem, G. (1983) Ruth's Song. *Ms. Magazines*, 46 (September) 47–50: 73–77.

Stevens, A. (2007) Survival of the Ideas that Fit: An Evolutionary Analogy for the Use of Evidence in Policy. *Social Policy and Society*, 6, 1: 25–35.

Stewart-Brown, S. and Shaw, R. (2002) Measuring the Parts Most Measures Do Not Reach. *Journal of Mental Health Promotion*, 1, 2: 4–10.

Sweeting, H. and West, P. (2002) Sex Differences in Health at Ages 11, 13 and 15. *Social and Medicine*, 56: 31–39.

Szasz, T. (1961) *The Myth of Mental Illness*, London: Paladin.

Szasz, T. (1970) *The Manufacture of Madness*, New York: Harper and Row.

Szasz, T. (1973) *The Age of Madness*, New York: Anchor Books.

Taylor, P. and Gunn, J. (1999) Violence and The Psychosis: Risk of Violence among Psychotic Men. *British Medical Journal*, 288: 1945–1949.

Tellias, D. (2001) Dual Diagnosis. *International Journal of Psychosocial Rehabilitation*, 5: 101–110. Accessed 15 January 2009.

The Mental Health Foundation (1997) *Knowing Our Own Minds: A Survey of How People in Emotional Distress Take Control of Their Own Lives*, London: The Mental Health Foundation.

The Mental Health Foundation (2001) *Turned Upside Down: Developing Community-Based Crisis Services for 16–25 Year Olds Experiencing a Mental Health Crisis*, London: The Mental Health Foundation.

The Mental Health Foundation (2007) *Listen Up! Person-Centred Approaches to Help Young People Experiencing Mental Health and Emotional Problems*, London: The Mental Health Foundation.

The Mental Health Foundation (2009) Latest Statistics Show Mental Health Must be Made National Priority, Says the Foundation at 60. http://www.mentalhealth.org.uk/media/news-releases-2009/3-february. Accessed 23 March 2010.

The NHS Confederation (2009) Key Facts and Trends in Mental Health, Accessed 28.03.2010 http://www.nhsconfed.org

Department of Health and Ageing (1996) The National Standards for Mental Health Services, National Mental Health Strategy, Canberra, The Australian Government.

Department of Health and Ageing (2002) The National Practice Standards for the Mental Health Workforce, National Mental Health Strategy, Canberra, The Australian Government.

Department of Health and Ageing (2010) The Revised National Standards for Mental Health Services, National Mental Health Strategy, Canberra, The Australian Government.

The Office for National Statistics (2005) *Mental Health in Children and Young People in Great Britain*, ONS.

The University of Queensland (2002) *Models of Service Provision to Adults with an Intellectual Disability with Co-existing Mental Disorder/Illness* (Dual Diagnosis), Queensland: Queensland Health and the Department of Premier and Cabinet.

Theriot, N. (1993) Women's Voices in Nineteenth-Century Medical Discourse: A Step Toward Deconstructing Science. *Signs*, 19: 1–31.

Thompson, N. (2006) *Anti-Discriminatory Practice*, 4th Edition, Basingstoke, Hampshire: Palgrave Macmillan.

Thompson, N. and Thompson, S. (2008) *The Critically Reflective Practitioner*, Basingstoke, Hampshire: Palgrave Macmillan.

Thornicroft, G. and Bebbington, P. (1989) Deinstitutionalization: From Hospital Closure to Service Development. *British Journal of Psychiatry*, 155: 739–753.

Timimi, S. (2002) *Pathological Child psychiatry and the Medicalisation of Childhood*, Sussex, UK: Brunner-Routledge.

Torsheim, T., Ravens-Sieberer, Y., Hetland, J. Valimaa, R., Danielson, M. and Overpeck, M. (2006) Cross-Nation Variation of Gender Differences in Adolescent Subjective Health in Europe and North America. *Social Science and Medicine*, 6: 815–827.

Triandis, H. C. (1995) *Individualism and Collectivism*, San Francisco: Westview.

Troll, L. (1983) Grandparents: The Family Watchdog, in T. H. Brubaker (Ed.) *Family Relationships in Later Life*, Sage: Beverley Hills.

Tse, T. and Howie, L. (2005) Adult Day Groups: Addressing Older People's Needs for Activity and Companionship. *Australia's Journal Ageing*, 24, 3, September: 134–140.

Tucker, J. S. (1991) Premenstrual Syndrome. *International Journal of Psychiatry in Medicine*, 21, 4: 319–324.

Tyrer, P. and Steinberg, D. (2003) *Models for Mental Disorders: Conceptual Models in Psychiatry*, Chichester: John Wiley and Sons.

Ungvari, G. S. and Chiu, H. F. K. (2004) The State of Psychiatry in Hong Kong: A Bird's Eye View. *International Journal of Social Psychiatry*, 50, 1: 5–9.

United Nations General Assembly (1992) *Principles for the Protection of Persons with Mental Illness and for the Improvement of Mental Health Care*, New York, United Nations.

Ussher, J. (1991) *Women's Madness: Misogyny or Mental Illness?* Hemel Hempstead: Harvester Wheatsheaf.

Van Den Tillaart, S., Kurtz, D. and Cash, P. (2009) Powerlessness, Marginalized Identity, and Silencing of Health Concerns: Voiced Realities of Women Living with a Mental Health Diagnosis. *International Journal of Mental Health Nursing*, 18: 153–153.

Vasas, E. R. (2005) Examining the Margins: A Concept Analysis of Marginalization. *Advances in Nursing Science*, 28, 3: 194–202.

Vaughn, C. and Leff, J. (1976) The Measurement of Expressed Emotion in the Families of Psychiatric Patients. *British Journal of Social and Clinical Psychology*, 15, 2: 157–165.

Veith, I. (1965) *Hysteria: The History of a Disease*. Chicago: University of Chicago Press.

Vicary, D. and Westerman, T. (2004) 'That's Just the Way He Is': Some Implications of Aboriginal Mental Health Beliefs. *Australian e-Journal for the Advancement of Mental Health*, 3, 3: 1–10.

Vostanis, P. (2007) Mental health and mental disorders, in J. Coleman and A. Hagell Adolescence (Eds) *Risk and Resilience: Against the Odds*, Chichester: John Wiley and Sons: 89–106.

Wakefield, J. C. (1992) The Concept of Mental Disorder. On the Boundary between Biological Facts and Social Values. *American Psychologist*, 47, 373–388.

Wall, S., Chruchill, R., Hotopf, M., Buchanan, A. and Wessely, S. (1999) *A Systematic Review of Research Relating to the Mental Health Act 1983*, London: Department of Health.

Warner, J. (2008) Community Care, Risk and the Shifting Locus of Danger and Vulnerability in Mental Health, in A. Petersen and I. Wilkinson (Eds), *Health, Risk and Vulnerability*, London: Routledge.

Wasow, M. (1995) *The Skipping Stone. Science and Behavior Books*, CA: Palo Alto.

Westermeyer, J. and Janca, A. (1997) Language Culture, and Psychopathology: Conceptual and Methodological Issues. *Transcultural Psychiatry*, 34: 291–311.

White, P., Chant, D., Edwards, N., Townsend, C. and Waghorn, G. (2005) Prevalence of Intellectual Disability and Comorbid Mental Disorder/Illness in an Australian Community Sample. *Australian and New Zealand Journal of Psychiatry*, May, 39: 395–400.

Whiteford, H., Thompson, I. and Casey, D. (2000) The Australian Mental Health System. *International Journal of Law and Psychiatry*, 23, 3–4: 403–417.

Williams, F. (1996) Postmodernism, Feminism and the Question of Difference, in N. Parton (Ed), *Social Theory, Social Change and Social Work*, London: Routledge.

Williams, F. (2001) In and Beyond New Labour: Towards a New Political Ethics of Care. *Critical Social Policy*, 21, 4, Issue 69: 467–494.

Williams, J. (2002) Social Inequalities and Mental Health, in C. Newnes, G. Holmes and C. Dunn (Eds), *This is Madness*, Llangarron: PCCS Books.

Williams, J. and Watson, G. (1996) Mental Health Services That Empower Women, in T. Heller, J. Reynold, R. Gomm, R. Muston and S. Pattison, (Eds) *Mental Health Matters: A Reader*, London: Macmillan, Open University.

Williams, J., Watson, G., Smith, H., Copperman, J. and Wood, D. (1993) *Purchasing Effective Mental Health Service for Women: A Framework for Action*, London: MIND publications/Tizard Centre, Canterbury: University of Kent at Canterbury.

Wilson, A. and Beresford, P. (2002) Madness, Distress and Postmodernity: Putting the Record Straight, in M. Corker and T. Shakespeare (Eds), *Disability/Postmodernism: Embodying Disability Theory*, London: Continuum.

Wilson, M. (2001) Black Women and Mental Health: Working toward Inclusive Mental Health Services. *Feminist Review*, 68, 34–51.

World Health Organisation (2005) *Child and Adolescent Resources, Global Concerns, Implications for Future Action*, Geneva: WHO.

World Health Organization (1978) Declaration of Alma-Ata. Geneva: World Health Organization. International Conference on Primary health Care. Alma-Ata. http://www.who.int/publications/almaata_declaration_en.pdf. Accessed 14th 04 2010.

World Health Organization (1993) The ICE-10 Classification of Mental and Behavioural Disorders (Second Edition No.2) www.who.int/classifciations/icd/en/bluebook.pdf. Accessed 29 April 2010.

World Health Organization (2001) The World Health Report 2001 – Mental Health: New Understanding, New Hope. Geneva: 49–84.

World Health Organization (2003) Mental Health Legislation and Human Rights. Singapore. Accessed 29 March 2008.

World Health Organisation (2009a) What is Mental Health http://www.who.int. Accessed 22nd May 2010.

World Health Organization (2009b) Mental Health Atlas. http://www.who.int/mental health/evidence/atlas. Accessed 25 September 2009.

Wright, G. S. I. (2010) *The Medicalization of Behaviour in Children Diagnosed as Having Attention Deficit Hyperactivity Disorder*, PhD Thesis, Sydney: University of Sydney.

Xiao, S., Khan, M., Yoon, Y., Phillips, M., Thomkangkoon, P., Pirkis, J., Hendin, H. (2008) Improving Treatment in Asia of Depression and Other Disorders that Convey Suicide Risk. Suicide and Suicide Prevention in Asia, Chapter 8: 77–87. Accessed 16 June 2009.

Yip, K-S. (2004) Taoism and Its Impact on Mental Health of The Chinese Communities. *International Journal of Social Psychiatry*, 50, 1: 25–42.

Young Minds (2000) *Whose Crisis: Meeting the Needs of Children and Young People with Serious Mental Health Problems*, London: Young Minds.

Young Minds (2006) *A Call to Action: Commissioning Mental Health Services for 16–25 Year-Olds*, London: Young Minds.

Young Minds Stressed Out and Struggling Project (2004) www.youngmindsorg.uk/sos. Accessed April 23 2010.

Youth Affairs Council of South Australia (YACSA) (2006) *Getting through: Responding to Young People's Mental Health Issues in the Youth Sector*, Adelaide: Government of South Australia.

Yurkovich, E. E. and Lattergrass, I. (2008) Defining Health and Unhealthiness: Perceptions Held By Native American Indians with Persistent Mental Illness. *Mental Health, Religion and Culture*, 11, 5: 437–459.

Zubrick, S. R., Silburn, S. R., Lawrence, D. M., Mitrou, F. G., Dalby, R. B., Blair, E. M., Griffin, J., Milroy, H., DeMaio, J., Cox, A. and Li, J. (2005) *The Western Australian Aboriginal Child Health Survey: The Social and Emotional Wellbeing of Aboriginal Children and Young People*, Perth, W: Curtin University of Technology and Telethon Institute for Child Health Research.

Index